# MULTI-~~t~~ASKING

## Other *Baby Blues*® Books from Andrews McMeel Publishing

*Guess Who Didn't Take a Nap?*
*I Thought Labor Ended When the Baby Was Born*
*We Are Experiencing Parental Difficulties . . . Please Stand By*
*Night of the Living Dad*
*I Saw Elvis in My Ultrasound*
*One More and We're Outnumbered!*
*Check, Please . . .*
*Threats, Bribes & Videotape*
*If I'm a Stay-at-Home Mom, Why Am I Always in the Car?*
*Lift and Separate*
*I Shouldn't Have to Scream More Than Once!*
*Motherhood Is Not for Wimps*
*Baby Blues®: Unplugged*
*Dad to the Bone*
*Never a Dry Moment*
*Two Plus One Is Enough*
*Playdate: Category 5*
*Our Server Is Down*
*Something Chocolate This Way Comes*
*Briefcase Full of Baby Blues®*
*Night Shift*
*The Day Phonics Kicked In*
*My Space*
*The Natural Disorder of Things*
*We Were Here First*
*Ambushed! In the Family Room*
*Cut!*
*Eat, Cry, Poop*
*Scribbles at an Exhibition*
*Bedlam*
*Wetter, Louder, Stickier*
*No Yelling!*
*Gross!*
*Binge Parenting*
*Adult Time*
*Surviving the Great Indoors*
*Stink Eye*

### Treasuries

*The Super-Absorbent Biodegradable Family-Size Baby Blues®*
*Baby Blues®: Ten Years and Still in Diapers*
*Butt-Naked Baby Blues®*
*Wall-to-Wall Baby Blues®*
*Driving Under the Influence of Children*
*Framed!*
*X-Treme Parenting*
*BBXX: Baby Blues: Decades 1 and 2*
*BB3X: Baby Blues: The Third Decade*

### Gift Books

*It's a Boy*
*It's a Girl*

# MULTI-tASKING

rick kirkman
jerry scott

Collection

In memory of Tom Rowan,
who believed in us from the start.

R.K.
J.S.

I THINK I'LL GO TAKE A NICE BATH.
OKIE DOKIE.
ZZZT ZZZT

1-3

©2021, BABY BLUES BROS LLC DIST. BY KING FEATURES SYNDICATE
"NO CHRISTMAS FUDGE LEFT," HUH?
ARREST HER!
KIRKMAN & SCOTT

WHERE DOES ALL THIS LAUNDRY COME FROM?

PILES OF IT, EVERYWHERE I LOOK!

WHAT AM I, THE QUEEN OF LAUNDRY OR SOMETHINMBLL...

ZZZZZZ

**To be continued...**

©2021, BABY BLUES BROS LLC DIST. BY KING FEATURES SYNDICATE 1-4

KIRKMAN & SCOTT

SO I'M THE QUEEN OF LAUNDRY?
THAT'S RIGHT, YOUR MAJESTY.
I DON'T WANT TO BE QUEEN OF THAT! I WANT SOMETHING FUN! SEXY! COOL!
I WANT TO BE EMPEROR OF RELAXATION!
SORRY. THAT WENT TO A GUY.
KIRKMAN & SCOTT
©2021, BABY BLUES BROS LLC DIST. BY KING FEATURES SYNDICATE 1-6

BEHOLD! YOUR EMPIRE!
AACK!
I'M THE QUEEN OF LAUNDRY, SO I HAVE TO DO ALL OF THAT ALONE??
OF COURSE NOT, YOUR HIGHNESS, YOU'LL HAVE HELP FROM YOUR FAMILY.
MY FAMILY IS HERE, TOO?
PRESENTING THE ROYAL PAIN IN THE BUTT.
HI, MOM.
KIRKMAN & SCOTT
©2021, BABY BLUES BROS LLC DIST. BY KING FEATURES SYNDICATE 1-7

NO! I DON'T WANT TO BE THE QUEEN OF LAUNDRY!
WANDA? WAKE UP!
I HAD THIS DREAM WHERE I HAD TO DO LAUNDRY FOR A WHOLE KINGDOM!
HA! HA! THAT'S CRAZY!
WHERE DO THESE WEIRD IDEAS COME FROM?
F.Y.I., I'M OUT OF CLEAN UNDERWEAR.
©2021, BABY BLUES BROS LLC DIST. BY KING FEATURES SYNDICATE 1-8
KIRKMAN & SCOTT

DAD, I NEED SOME ADVICE.
GOOD, SOLID, DOWN-TO-EARTH ADVICE.
HOW CAN I HELP?
TELL ME WHERE I CAN FIND MOM.
©2021, BABY BLUES BROS LLC DIST. BY KING FEATURES SYNDICATE 1-9
KIRKMAN & SCOTT

ONCE AGAIN, DAD-MAN SAVES THE DAY!
VERY IMPRESSIVE.
YAY! DAD-MAN!

DARRYL, CAN YOU OPEN THIS?

STAND ASIDE, CITIZEN!
KIRKMAN & SCOTT

GAAAA
POP!
1-10

ONCE AGAIN, DAD-MAN SAVES THE DAY!
VERY IMPRESSIVE.
YAY! DAD-MAN!
©2021, BABY BLUES BROS LLC DIST. BY KING FEATURES SYNDICATE

IF ONLY YOUR SUPER POWERS INCLUDED LIFTING THE TOILET SEAT.
EVEN SUPERHEROES HAVE LIMITATIONS.

I'M GOING FOR A RUN.
THAT'S THE THIRD TIME THIS WEEK!
YOU'RE REALLY TRYING TO WORK OFF THAT DAD BOD, AREN'T YOU?
I AM NOW.
©2021, BABY BLUES BROS LLC DIST. BY KING FEATURES SYNDICATE 1-11
KIRKMAN & SCOTT

OW!
WHAT?
I JUST HAD A STABBING PAIN IN MY LEFT FOOT.
IT'S PROBABLY FROM ALL THAT RUNNING YOU'VE BEEN DOING.
ARE YOU SAYING THAT I'M GETTING OLD?
DON'T SHOOT THE MESSENGER.
©2021, BABY BLUES BROS LLC DIST. BY KING FEATURES SYNDICATE 1-12
KIRKMAN & SCOTT

OW. OW. OW.
YOUR FOOT?

YEAH. IT HURTS WORSE TODAY.
KIRKMAN & SCOTT
©2021, BABY BLUES BROS LLC DIST. BY KING FEATURES SYNDICATE 1-13

DO YOU WANT ME TO CALL IN SICK FOR YOU?
MAKE IT SOUND HEROIC.

WHAT DO YOU THINK, BOB?
IT LOOKS LIKE JUST A DAMAGED TENDON.

YOU'LL WEAR A WALKING BOOT FOR A WEEK, AND IF IT'S NOT BETTER, WE'LL DO AN M.R.I.
KIRKMAN & SCOTT
©2021, BABY BLUES BROS LLC DIST. BY KING FEATURES SYNDICATE 1-14

OR WE CAN SKIP ALL THAT AND JUST PUT YOU DOWN.
I DON'T THINK MY INSURANCE WILL COVER IT.

WHAT'S THIS?
SOMETHING I HAVE TO WEAR UNTIL MY FOOT GETS BETTER.
THUNK! THUNK! THUNK!
IT'S CALLED A "WALKING BOOT."
THEY OUGHTA CALL IT A "THUNKING BOOT."
THUNK! THUNK! THUNK!
©2021, BABY BLUES BROS LLC DIST. BY KING FEATURES SYNDICATE 1-15
THANKS. RIDICULE HELPS.
AAAGH! IT'S FRANKENDAD!
THUNK! THUNK! THUNK!

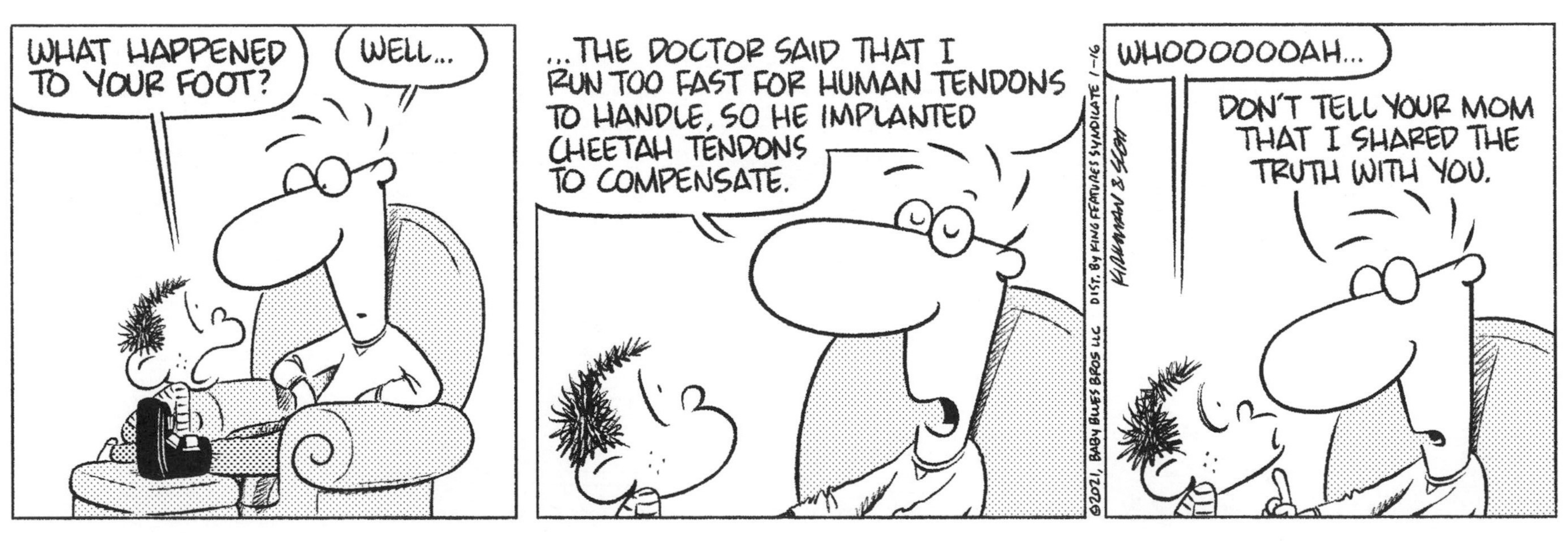
WHAT HAPPENED TO YOUR FOOT?
WELL...
...THE DOCTOR SAID THAT I RUN TOO FAST FOR HUMAN TENDONS TO HANDLE, SO HE IMPLANTED CHEETAH TENDONS TO COMPENSATE.
©2021, BABY BLUES BROS LLC DIST. BY KING FEATURES SYNDICATE 1-16
WHOOOOOOAH...
DON'T TELL YOUR MOM THAT I SHARED THE TRUTH WITH YOU.

I HAVE AN IDEA!

NOW ALL I HAVE TO DO IS PASTE THESE PICTURES ON THE TITLE PAGE.
HURRY UP! WE'RE GOING TO BE LATE!

GASP! WE'RE ALL OUT OF GLUE STICKS AND TAPE!
WE SHOULD BE IN THE CAR BY NOW!
©2021, BABY BLUES BROS LLC DIST. BY KING FEATURES SYNDICATE

I HAVE AN IDEA!

DID YOU FIND SOME GLUE?
NOPE. SOMETHING STICKIER.
RUB RUB RUB
1-17

THE TV REMOTE??
THESE THINGS ARE NEVER COMING OFF!
KIRKMAN & SCOTT

HOW'S YOUR FOOT TODAY?
OKAY, I GUESS.
CLOMP! CLOMP!

I'D HELP YOU WITH THE DISHES, BUT THIS DARN WALKING BOOT LIMITS MY MOBILITY.
KIRKMAN & SCOTT

I JUST HOPE I CAN DRAG IT ALL THE WAY BACK TO THE COUCH.
IT'S A WALKING BOOT, DARRYL, NOT AN IRON LUNG.
©2021, BABY BLUES BROS LLC DIST. BY KING FEATURES SYNDICATE 2-1

IS IT HARD TO WALK IN THIS BOOT, DAD?
IT'S PRETTY AWKWARD.

CAN YOU RUN?
HARDLY.
CAN YOU JUMP?
NO WAY.
©2021, BABY BLUES BROS LLC DIST. BY KING FEATURES SYNDICATE 2-2

WANT TO PLAY A LITTLE ONE-ON-ONE?
KIRKMAN & SCOTT

HOW'S OUR 401(k) LOOKING?
BLEAK.

C'MON! THAT'S NOT TRUE!
YEAH, YOU'RE RIGHT.
2-3
©2021, BABY BLUES BROS LLC DIST. BY KING FEATURES SYNDICATE

WE PASSED "BLEAK" ABOUT TWO KIDS AGO.
KIRKMAN & SCOTT

ARE YOU STILL IN LOVE WITH YOUR TEACHER?
YEAH, BUT SHE BARELY NOTICES ME.

BE FUNNY! GIRLS LOVE A GUY WHO CAN MAKE THEM LAUGH.
2-4
©2021, BABY BLUES BROS LLC DIST. BY KING FEATURES SYNDICATE

YOU TOLD MS. SHULKIN TO PULL YOUR FINGER??
IT WAS ZOE'S IDEA!
KIRKMAN & SCOTT

I'M HOME!
IS IT STILL RAINING?

IT SURE IS!
I'M NOT GOING TO COME OUT THERE AND FIND YOUR WET RAINCOAT AND MUDDY BOOTS ON THE FLOOR, AM I?

HOW LONG HAVE WE KNOWN EACH OTHER, MOM?
KIRKMAN & SCOTT
©2021, BABY BLUES BROS LLC DIST. BY KING FEATURES SYNDICATE 2-5

IS IT GOING TO LEAVE A HORRIBLE SCAR THAT WILL SICKEN OTHERS WHEN THEY SEE IT?
IT'S JUST A SCRAPE.

I'LL CLEAN IT UP, PATCH YOUR JEANS, AND IT'LL BE LIKE IT NEVER HAPPENED.
©2021, BABY BLUES BROS LLC DIST. BY KING FEATURES SYNDICATE 2-6

YOU SURE KNOW HOW TO TAKE ALL THE FUN OUT OF HAVING A BLOODY KNEE!
KIRKMAN & SCOTT

EWW.

KIRKMAN & SCOTT

1-24



I GUESS ANOTHER YEAR'S WORTH OF EXPERIENCE HAS TO WEIGH SOMETHING.

I'D SAY AROUND TEN POUNDS.

©2021, BABY BLUES BROS LLC DIST. BY KING FEATURES SYNDICATE 2-8
THE HAMDALORIAN!
KIRKMAN & SCOTT

HAMMIE, WHAT ARE YOU DOING?
NOT HAMMIE, THE HAMDALORIAN.
EECHH! P-TOOIE!
©2021, BABY BLUES BROS LLC DIST. BY KING FEATURES SYNDICATE 2-9
FORGOT TO RINSE THE SAND OUT OF THE BUCKET FIRST?
PERHAPS.
KIRKMAN & SCOTT

IDENTITY, PLEASE.
YOUR DAD.

PROVIDER, MENTOR, SOOTHER, TEACHER, ROLE MODEL...
OKAY, OKAY.
KIRKMAN & SCOTT
©2021, BABY BLUES BROS LLC DIST. BY KING FEATURES SYNDICATE 2-10
NEXT TIME, JUST A NAME, NOT YOUR RÉSUMÉ.

HAMMIE, NO HELMETS AT THE DINNER TABLE.
KIRKMAN & SCOTT

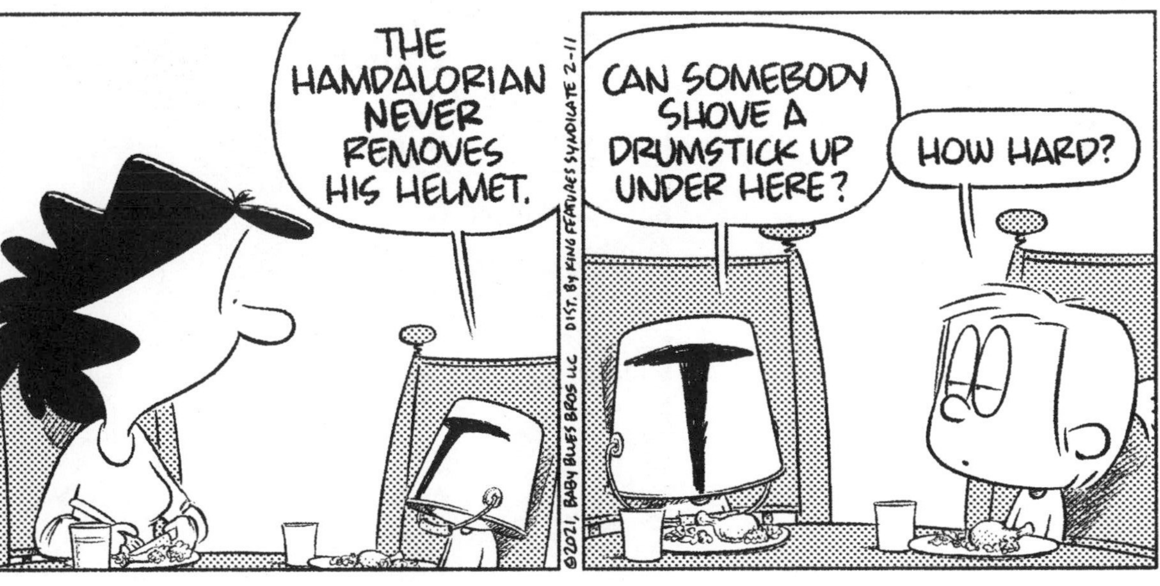
THE HAMDALORIAN NEVER REMOVES HIS HELMET.
©2021, BABY BLUES BROS LLC DIST. BY KING FEATURES SYNDICATE 2-11
CAN SOMEBODY SHOVE A DRUMSTICK UP UNDER HERE?
HOW HARD?

HAPPY VALENTINE'S DAY, DARRYL.
HAPPY VALENTINE'S DAY, WANDA.

IN FACT, I DON'T THINK I COULD LOVE YOU MORE.
2-14

I LOVE YOU.
I LOVE YOU, TOO.

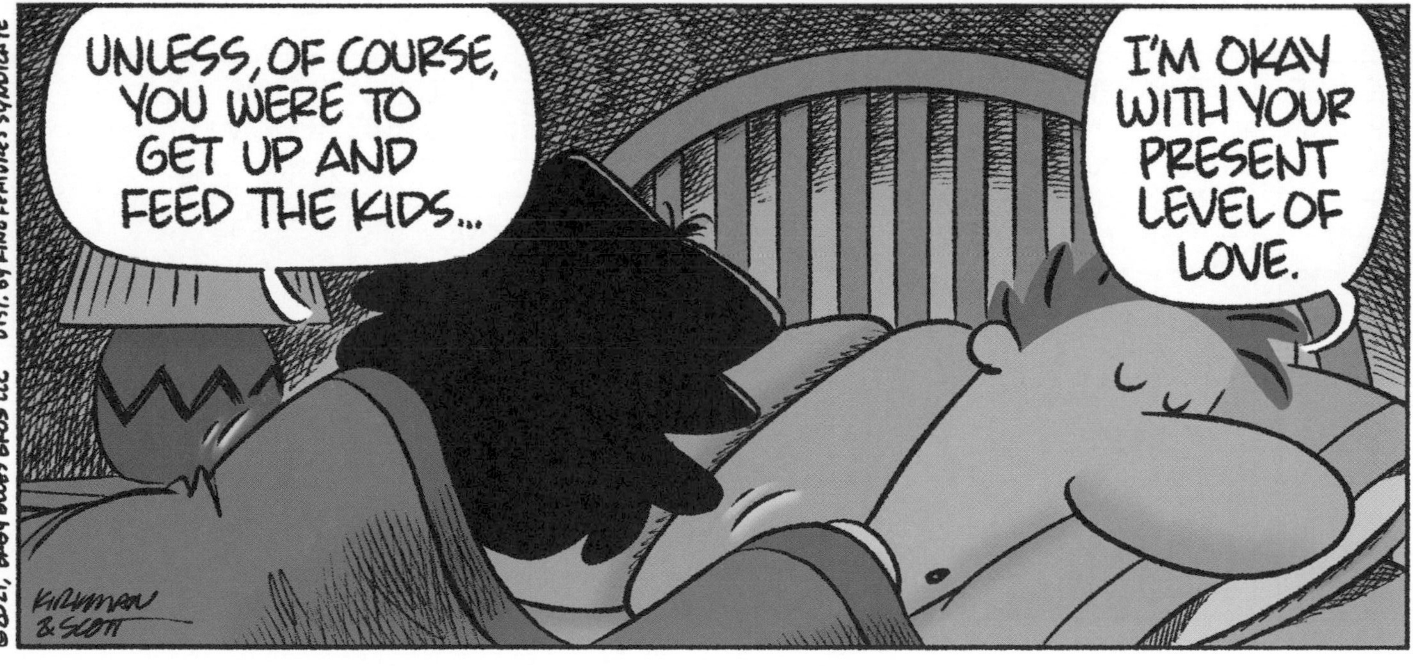
UNLESS, OF COURSE, YOU WERE TO GET UP AND FEED THE KIDS...
I'M OKAY WITH YOUR PRESENT LEVEL OF LOVE.
KIRKMAN & SCOTT

WHAT DO YOU WANT, HAMDALORIAN?
WE HAVE BEEN SUMMONED.
LEAD THE WAY TO THE ONE KNOWN AS "MOTHER."
NO PROBLEM.
OH, AND WATCH YOUR STEP.
THE HAMDALORIAN WISHES HE HAD HIS BLASTER HANDY.
©2021, BABY BLUES BROS LLC DIST. BY KING FEATURES SYNDICATE 2-12
KIRKMAN & SCOTT

GREETINGS, EARTH WOMAN.
I'VE HAD ENOUGH OF THE HAMDALORIAN ACT, MISTER.
KIRKMAN & SCOTT
TAKE THAT THING OFF.
THE HAMDALORIAN DOES NOT REMOVE HIS HELMET.
HE DOES THE NEXT TIME HE USES THE BATHROOM!
AFFIRMATIVE.
©2021, BABY BLUES BROS LLC DIST. BY KING FEATURES SYNDICATE 2-13

KIRKMAN & SCOTT
©2021, BABY BLUES BROS LLC DIST. BY KING FEATURES SYNDICATE 2-15

SOMETHING VE-R-R-R-R-Y SUSPICIOUS IS GOING ON IN THERE.
SILENCE?

I GOT AN EMAIL FROM A COMPANY THAT WANTS TO SPONSOR MY YOUTUBE CHANNEL.

HERE'S WHAT THEY'RE OFFERING.
©2021, BABY BLUES BROS LLC DIST. BY KING FEATURES SYNDICATE 2-16

KIRKMAN & SCOTT
THAT'S MORE THAN I MAKE!
YEAH. I'M EXCITED, TOO!

WANDA, WITH A TOY COMPANY SPONSORING YOUR VIDEOS, OUR MONEY WORRIES ARE OVER!
WELL, I WANT TO SEE THEIR PRODUCT FIRST BEFORE I JUST TAKE THE CASH.
YOUR INTEGRITY IS THREATENING MY JET SKI.
SORRY.
KIRKMAN & SCOTT
©2021, BABY BLUES BROS LLC DIST. BY KING FEATURES SYNDICATE 2-17

HERE'S THE TOY THE SPONSOR SENT ME TO CHECK OUT.
A STUFFED DOG?
IT'S AN A.I. PET. IT KNOWS COMMANDS, OBEYS AND INTERACTS WELL WITH PEOPLE.
IMAGINE A TOY WITH BETTER MANNERS THAN OUR KIDS.
NOT EVEN A STRETCH.
OW! GIVE IT! SCRAM!
KIRKMAN & SCOTT
©2021, BABY BLUES BROS LLC DIST. BY KING FEATURES SYNDICATE 2-18

GUYS, I WANT YOU TO DO ME A FAVOR.
KIRKMAN & SCOTT

I MIGHT DO BUSINESS WITH THE COMPANY THAT MAKES THIS TOY, AND I WANT TO KNOW IF IT'S ANY GOOD.
©2021, BABY BLUES BROS LLC DIST. BY KING FEATURES SYNDICATE 2-19

PERMISSION TO GO FULL HAMMIE ON IT?
GRANTED.
RUN, PLASTIC DOG! RUN!!

WELL, I TURNED THE SPONSORSHIP DOWN.
WHAT? WHY??

I FOUND OUT THAT THEIR TOYS ARE MADE OF ASBESTOS AND LEAD BY SLAVE LABOR IN A PRISON CAMP FOR TODDLERS.
KIRKMAN & SCOTT
©2021, BABY BLUES BROS LLC DIST. BY KING FEATURES SYNDICATE 2-20

LET'S NOT RUSH TO JUDGMENT HERE.
DARRYL!

GET UP!

EAT UP!

HURRY UP!

STUDY UP!
CLAM UP!
SIT UP!

FINISH UP!
TIDY UP!
CLEAN UP!
BRUSH UP!

2-21

©2021, BABY BLUES BROS LLC DIST. BY KING FEATURES SYNDICATE

FED UP?

STRAIGHT UP.

KIRKMAN & SCOTT

I GOT AN EMAIL TODAY ABOUT SOCCER REGISTRATION.
ALREADY?
KIRKMAN & SCOTT

IT'S FOR THE EARLYBIRD SPRING WARMUP COED SEASON.
©2021, BABY BLUES BROS LLC DIST. BY KING FEATURES SYNDICATE 2-22
THEY WON'T BE HAPPY UNTIL THEY HAVE **ALL** OF OUR MONEY.
AT LEAST THEY'RE UPFRONT ABOUT IT.

WELL, I GOT ZOE AND HAMMIE SIGNED UP FOR SOCCER.

HAMMIE IS OLD ENOUGH THAT HE AND ZOE COULD END UP ON THE SAME TEAM.
©2021, BABY BLUES BROS LLC DIST. BY KING FEATURES SYNDICATE 2-23

**ONE** PRACTICE TO DRIVE TO? **ONE** GAME TO ATTEND?
IT'S THE STUFF DREAMS ARE MADE OF!
KIRKMAN & SCOTT

MOM, I NEED ONE OF DAD'S OLD SWEATSHIRTS AND A THICK MARKER.
AND WHY?
HE WANTS TO HELP ZOE AND ME WITH SOCCER DRILLS, SO I WANT TO MAKE HIM A "COACH" SHIRT.
KIRKMAN & SCOTT
©2021, BABY BLUES BROS LLC DIST. BY KING FEATURES SYNDICATE 2-24
YOU COULDN'T HAVE HAD ZOE HELP WITH THE SPELLING?
IF THE SHIRT FITS...
COUCH

HOW DID THE KIDS' SOCCER TRYOUTS GO TODAY?
FINE.
DID HAMMIE AND ZOE END UP ON THE SAME TEAM?
YUP...
©2021, BABY BLUES BROS LLC DIST. BY KING FEATURES SYNDICATE 2-25
KIRKMAN & SCOTT
...AND THE TEAM BONDING IS ALREADY UNDERWAY.
NO! NO! NO! NO!
THIS IS THE WORST DAY OF MY LIFE!!

PASS ME THE BALL!
SHUT UP!

I'M OPEN!
SO AM I! SHUT UP!
©2021, BABY BLUES BROS LLC DIST. BY KING FEATURES SYNDICATE 2-26

I SEE ANOTHER MEETING WITH THE COACH COMING.
ONLY FOURTEEN MORE GAMES.
YOU SHUT UP!
NO, YOU SHUT UP!
KIRKMAN & SCOTT

HAMMIE! ARE THESE VALENTINES YOU MADE FOR SCHOOL?
OH, NO! I FORGOT TO PASS THEM OUT!

SO NOBODY GOT A VALENTINE FROM YOU.
I GUESS NOT.
©2021, BABY BLUES BROS LLC DIST. BY KING FEATURES SYNDICATE 2-27

AND YOU SIGNED THEM ALL: "EDA BOOGER."
THAT'S THE REAL TRAGEDY, IF YOU ASK ME.
KIRKMAN & SCOTT

I'M GOING TO LOSE TEN POUNDS NEXT MONTH.
I BELIEVE YOU WILL.

PLUS, I'LL RE-DO ALL OF THE FLOWERBEDS, TACKLE THE STORAGE CLOSET AND PAINT THE GARAGE FLOOR!
WOW!

I'M ALSO GOING TO GET ALL OF OUR PHOTOS ORGANIZED!
GO FOR IT!

AND I'M REALLY GOING TO EMBRACE DISTANCE LEARNING.
NOW YOU'RE SOUNDING DELUSIONAL.
KIRKMAN & SCOTT

I GOT A NOTE FROM THE PEDIATRICIAN.
MM.

THE KIDS NEED TO GET VACCINATED, SO YOU NEED TO HELP ME THINK OF A WAY TO TELL THEM.

SORRY. I GOTTA GET THIS.
YOUR PHONE DIDN'T EVEN RING, YOU COWARD!
KIRKMAN & SCOTT
©2021, BABY BLUES BROS LLC DIST. BY KING FEATURES SYNDICATE 3-1

YOU NEED TO COME STRAIGHT TO THE PICKUP AREA AFTER SCHOOL.
WHY?

OH, THERE'S JUST A LITTLE BUSINESS WE HAVE TO DO.

I BET THEY FINALLY FOUND A FAMILY TO ADOPT YOU.
I HOPE THEY'RE WOLVES!
KIRKMAN & SCOTT
©2021, BABY BLUES BROS LLC DIST. BY KING FEATURES SYNDICATE 3-2

WHERE ARE WE GOING?
OH, JUST TO AN APPOINTMENT.

WHAT KIND OF AN APPOINTMENT?
OH, YOU KNOW... THE UM... INJECTION KIND.
©2021, BABY BLUES BROS LLC DIST. BY KING FEATURES SYNDICATE 3-3

AAAUGGGHHH!
IT'S A TRAP! ABANDON SHIP!
IT'S A VACCINATION, NOT AN AMPUTATION!
KIRKMAN & SCOTT

HEY! THIS IS THE DOCTOR'S OFFICE! YOU LIED TO US!
KIRKMAN & SCOTT

I DIDN'T LIE...I JUST SORT OF FUDGED FACTS A LITTLE.
©2021, BABY BLUES BROS LLC DIST. BY KING FEATURES SYNDICATE 3-4

NO FAIR.
I HATE IT WHEN THEY LEARN OUR SKILLS.

I'M HOME, SWEETIE!
THE TOILET'S CLOGGED, THE SINK IS BACKED UP, AND I'M THIS CLOSE TO SENTENCING YOUR SON TO LIFE IN TIME OUT WITHOUT PAROLE.
DOES THIS MEAN THE HONEYMOON IS OVER?
JUST PLUNGE.
©2021, BABY BLUES BROS LLC DIST. BY KING FEATURES SYNDICATE 3-5
KIRKMAN & SCOTT

DID YOU GET THE TOILET FIXED?
TOO EARLY TO TELL.
THAT SOUNDS LIKE A "NO."
NOT NECESSARILY...
SOMETIMES THESE THINGS HEAL THEMSELVES.
THAT'S YOUR PLAN? HOPING FOR A TOILET MIRACLE?
©2021, BABY BLUES BROS LLC DIST. BY KING FEATURES SYNDICATE 3-6
KIRKMAN & SCOTT

ARE YOU GONNA SQUASH THE SPIDER?
MAYBE WE CAN CATCH IT AND LET IT GO.
REALLY?
YEAH, THIS IS JUST A HARMLESS DADDY LONGLEGS.
SEE HOW EASY IT IS TO SHOW A LITTLE KINDNESS?
THERE YOU GO, LITTLE SPI-
WHERE'D HE GO?
IS IT ON ME?
GET IT OFF! GET IT OFF! GET IT OFF!
EEEEEEEK!
SLAP! SLAP! SLAP!
SLAP! SLAP! SLAP! SLAP!
DID YOU RESCUE THE SPIDER?
IF WE DIDN'T, IT WAS A CLEAR CASE OF SELF-DEFENSE.

ARE YOU COMING TO MY GAME?
IT DEPENDS.
WILL A BEE FLY UP YOUR SLEEVE, CAUSING YOU TO JUMP AROUND UNTIL YOUR PANTS FALL DOWN SO THAT YOU DROP THE BALL AND LOSE THE GAME?
©2021, BABY BLUES BROS LLC DIST. BY KING FEATURES SYNDICATE 3-8
NO.
TOO BAD. I'D GO SEE THAT.
KIRKMAN & SCOTT

GO, HAMMIE, GO!
RUN, BUDDY!!
HUSTLE! HUSTLE!
YOU CAN MAKE IT!!
©2021, BABY BLUES BROS LLC DIST. BY KING FEATURES SYNDICATE 3-9
GOOD THING THE BATHROOM IS CLOSE.
HE SHOULD CUT BACK ON THE GATORADE.
KIRKMAN & SCOTT

YOU COULDN'T HIT A BEACH BALL, BATTER!

YOU THROW LIKE MY GRANDMA! CINDERELLA GETS TO THE BALL FASTER THAN YOU!

©2021, BABY BLUES BROS LLC DIST. BY KING FEATURES SYNDICATE 3-10
YOU CAN STOP HECKLING HIM, ZOE. THE GAME'S OVER.
KIRKMAN & SCOTT
I DIDN'T WANT TO WASTE THESE.

SEE, I MULTIPLIED ALL OF MY ANSWERS BY ZERO.
WHY?

DUH! BECAUSE THAT MAKES ALL THE ANSWERS ZERO, SO I'M NEVER WRONG!
KIRKMAN & SCOTT
©2021, BABY BLUES BROS LLC DIST. BY KING FEATURES SYNDICATE 3-11
I CAN'T WAIT TO SEE MY GRADE!
YOU'VE ALREADY SEEN IT!

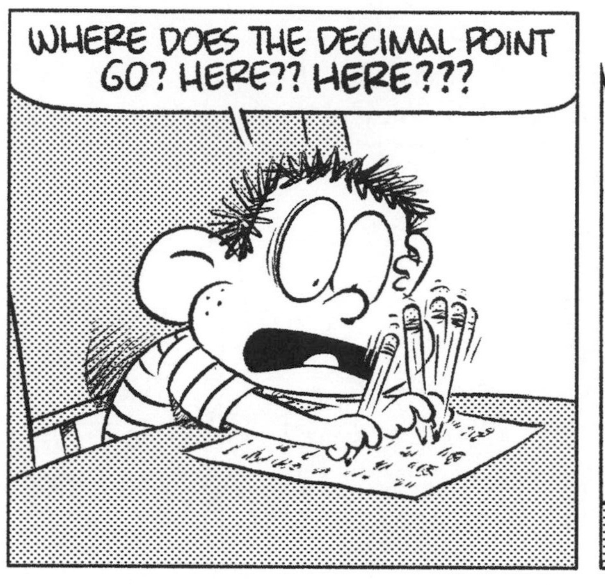
WHERE DOES THE DECIMAL POINT GO? HERE?? HERE???

WHY NOT HERE? OR HERE? HERE? HERE? HERE?...
JAB! JAB! JAB! JAB!
JAB! JAB! JAB! JAB! JAB!
©2021, BABY BLUES BROS LLC DIST. BY KING FEATURES SYNDICATE 3-12

I CAN'T WAIT FOR THE STORY BEHIND THIS.
YOU'RE NEXT, FRACTIONS!
KIRKMAN & SCOTT

SO I WAS PUTTING MY UNDIES IN THE HAMPER WHEN I NOTICED A DISGUSTING—
HAMMIE! WE'RE EATING!

I KNOW! I WASN'T GOING TO DESCRIBE IT!
KIRKMAN & SCOTT

THAT'S WHY I TOOK THE PICTURE.
BREAKFAST OVER.
©2021, BABY BLUES BROS LLC DIST. BY KING FEATURES SYNDICATE 3-13

C'MON, DAD! YOU SAID WE COULD GO KITE-FLYING TODAY!

I KNOW I DID, BUT IT'S POURING OUTSIDE.

©2021, BABY BLUES BROS LLC DIST. BY KING FEATURES SYNDICATE

YOU'RE A GOOD DADDY.

REMEMBER THAT WHEN YOU SEE THE ELECTRIC BILL.

3-14

KIRKMAN & SCOTT

GUESS WHAT? OUR CLASS IS GOING TO MAKE A TIME CAPSULE!
THAT SOUNDS FUN.

YEAH, AND WE ALL GET TO CHOOSE ONE THING TO BURY IN IT FOR TEN YEARS!
©2021, BABY BLUES BROS LLC DIST. BY KING FEATURES SYNDICATE 3-15

YOUR BROTHER WON'T FIT INSIDE.
WE WON'T KNOW THAT UNTIL WE TRY.
KIRKMAN & SCOTT

HEY, HOW'S YOUR CLASS TIME CAPSULE COMING ALONG?
WELL?

THE ITEMS WE PUT IN IT ARE SUPPOSED TO REFLECT THE TIMES WE LIVE IN, RIGHT?
RIGHT...
KIRKMAN & SCOTT
©2021, BABY BLUES BROS LLC DIST. BY KING FEATURES SYNDICATE 3-16

SO FAR, IT HAS THIRTY MASKS.

I SOLVED YOUR TIME CAPSULE PROBLEM.
IS THAT SO?

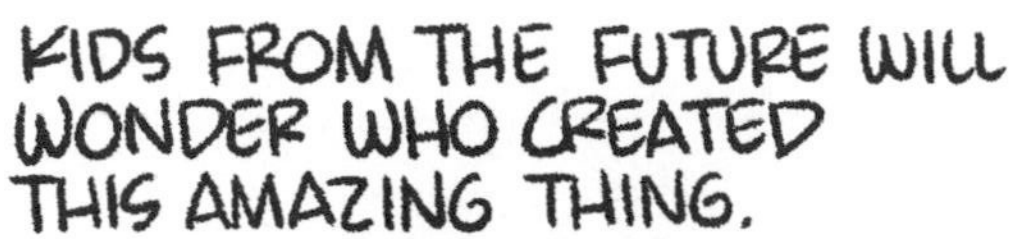
KIDS FROM THE FUTURE WILL WONDER WHO CREATED THIS AMAZING THING.

©2021, BABY BLUES BROS LLC DIST. BY KING FEATURES SYNDICATE 3-17
THAT LOOKS LIKE A GIANT BOOGER.
WRAPPED IN FOIL TO PRESERVE FRESHNESS!
KIRKMAN & SCOTT

WHAT ARE YOU PUTTING IN THE TIME CAPSULE, KEESHA?
I'M NOT SURE.

THERE'S A LOT OF PRESSURE TO COME UP WITH SOMETHING GOOD.
TELL ME ABOUT IT.
KIRKMAN & SCOTT

©2021, BABY BLUES BROS LLC DIST. BY KING FEATURES SYNDICATE 3-18
I MISS THIRD GRADE.
SIGH! THOSE WERE THE DAYS.

WELL, WE BURIED OUR TIME CAPSULE TODAY.
WHAT DID YOU DECIDE TO CONTRIBUTE?
MONEY. IN TEN YEARS, PEOPLE WILL BE USING THEIR PHONES TO BUY EVERYTHING, AND CASH WON'T BE USEFUL.
INTERESTING!
I KNOW, JUST DON'T TELL DAD.
HAS ANYBODY SEEN MY WALLET?
©2021, BABY BLUES BROS LLC DIST. BY KING FEATURES SYNDICATE 3-19
KIRKMAN & SCOTT

OKAY, WREN, LET'S SEE WHAT'S ON OUR SHOPPING LIST.
DONUTS. DONUTS. DONUTS. DONUTS. DONUTS. DONUTS. ICE CREAM.
YOU'RE NOT ALLOWED TO TALK TO SIRI ANYMORE.
BUT SHE LISTENS TO ME!
©2021, BABY BLUES BROS LLC DIST. BY KING FEATURES SYNDICATE 3-20
KIRKMAN & SCOTT

SO, HOW ARE YOU GUYS HOLDING UP, WANDA?

GOOD, I GUESS. YOU?

3-21

GOOD. HOW WAS YOUR WEEKEND?

FINE. EXCEPT THAT HAMMIE HAS BEEN DRIVING ME NUTS WITH THAT UKULELE OF HIS.

WHAT DO YOU MEAN?

HE CAN MAKE UP A SONG ABOUT ANYTHING!

KIRKMAN & SCOTT

THIS MORNING, HE WROTE ONE ABOUT ZOE EATING A POP-TART.

SO?



GUESS WHAT CONVENIENTLY RHYMES WITH "TART."

DID SOMEONE REQUEST MY BREAKFAST SONG?

©2021, BABY BLUES BROS LLC DIST. BY KING FEATURES SYNDICATE 3-22
NAW.
KIRKMAN & SCOTT

©2021, BABY BLUES BROS LLC DIST. BY KING FEATURES SYNDICATE 3-23
THEY WOULDN'T DARE.
KIRKMAN & SCOTT

OKAY, COUNTERTOP TO TABLE, TABLE TO HIGH CHAIR, AND DISMOUNT WITH A FLIP.
MOM'S GONNA KILL US.

THE ONLY WAY SHE'S GONNA KNOW IS IF SOMEBODY TELLS HER!
EXACTLY.
©2021, BABY BLUES BROS LLC DIST. BY KING FEATURES SYNDICATE 3-24

NEVER PLAY WITH A SERIAL TATTLER.
WHAT IF I TOLD ON US, BUT DIDN'T USE OUR REAL NAMES?
KIRKMAN & SCOTT

ZOE...
WE DID IT! I ADMIT IT!

WE MADE AN INDOOR PARKOUR COURSE AND JUMPED OFF ALL THE FURNITURE AND PROBABLY WRECKED SOME STUFF BUT IT WAS ALL HAMMIE'S IDEA WE'RE GUILTY GUILTY GUILTY!
©2021, BABY BLUES BROS LLC DIST. BY KING FEATURES SYNDICATE 3-25

...UNLESS THAT WASN'T WHAT YOU WANTED TO TALK TO ME ABOUT.
TIMEOUT, HERE I COME.
KIRKMAN & SCOTT

THEY WERE GOING TO JUMP FROM THE COUCH TO THE EXERCISE BALL, BOUNCE UP...
...GRAB A CEILING FAN BLADE, MAKE ONE FULL REVOLUTION AND CANNONBALL INTO THIS PAIL OF WATER!
THAT'S CRAZY!
©2021, BABY BLUES BROS LLC DIST. BY KING FEATURES SYNDICATE 3-26
KIRKMAN & SCOTT
ALL I DID WAS SIT IN BUDGET MEETINGS ALL DAY.
YOU'RE SUPPOSED TO SYMPATHIZE WITH ME, NOT ENVY THEM.

THE SHOW IS CALLED "SPACE MAGGOTS," WHICH IS BASICALLY WHAT IT'S ABOUT.
TELL ME MORE.
...AND THEY END UP FEEDING ON ASTRONAUT GUTS, WHICH EXPLAINS ALL THE EMPTY SPACE SUITS FLOATING AROUND IN SPACE.
OKAY. THANKS.
©2021, BABY BLUES BROS LLC DIST. BY KING FEATURES SYNDICATE 3-27
MOM IS ACTUALLY INTERESTED IN "SPACE MAGGOTS"?
NAW. IT JUST HELPS HER TO STOP SNACKING.
KIRKMAN & SCOTT

WE ACCIDENTALLY GOT SOME OF MIKE AND YOLANDA'S MAIL. I'LL BE BACK IN TWO SECONDS.

ZOE, YOU'RE IN CHARGE.



HOW ON EARTH...?

I'VE BEEN TRAINING FOR THIS MOMENT MY WHOLE LIFE.

KIRKMAN & SCOTT 3-28

HEY! STAN IS IN TOWN!
STAN? YOUR OLD ROOMMATE?
YEAH! REMEMBER GOOD OLD STAN?
OF COURSE I DO.
YOU DON'T FORGET PEOPLE WHO THROW UP ON YOUR SHOES. TWICE.
OH YEAH.
KIRKMAN & SCOTT
©2021, BABY BLUES BROS LLC DIST. BY KING FEATURES SYNDICATE 3-29

I CAN'T BELIEVE YOU INVITED STAN FOR DINNER.
LOOK, I KNOW HE WAS A LITTLE WILD IN COLLEGE...
©2021, BABY BLUES BROS LLC DIST. BY KING FEATURES SYNDICATE 3-30
...BUT FROM WHAT I HEAR, HE'S MELLOWED OUT, JUST LIKE THE REST OF US.
HONK! HONK!
PAR-TAY!
TELL ME MORE.
KIRKMAN & SCOTT

WELL, "GOOD OL' STAN" HASN'T CHANGED A BIT.
COME ON, WANDA, GIVE HIM A CHANCE!

NONE OF US ARE THE SAME KNUCKLEHEADS TODAY THAT WE WERE IN COLLEGE.
BZZZZZZ
KIRKMAN & SCOTT
©2021, BABY BLUES BROS LLC DIST. BY KING FEATURES SYNDICATE 3-31

WEDGIE!!
GLAD TO HEAR IT.

KIDS, THIS IS STAN. WE WENT TO COLLEGE TOGETHER.
THREE KIDS! WOW!

YOU'VE BEEN BUSY, MacPHERSON!
©2021, BABY BLUES BROS LLC DIST. BY KING FEATURES SYNDICATE 4-1

BUSY WITH WHAT?
DINNERTIME! GO WASH UP!
KIRKMAN & SCOTT

MORE WINE, WILD WANDA?
NO, THANK YOU, STAN.
WILD WANDA?
©2021, BABY BLUES BROS LLC DIST. BY KING FEATURES SYNDICATE 4-2
KIRKMAN & SCOTT
INTERESTING!
THAT MEANS THAT SHE WAS ONCE FUN.
I'M STILL FUN!
I'M GLAD YOU GOT TO SEE STAN AGAIN.
YEAH. HE'S STILL CRAZY.
I CAN'T BELIEVE SOME OF THE STUNTS WE PULLED IN COLLEGE!
©2021, BABY BLUES BROS LLC DIST. BY KING FEATURES SYNDICATE 4-3
KIRKMAN & SCOTT
DETAILS, BUT NO BIG WORDS, OKAY?

SIGH! WHAT WAS THE EASTER BUNNY THINKING?

YOU MEAN THE SUPER-SOAKERS IN THE BASKETS!

MAYBE HE WAS THINKING THE KIDS SHOULD HAVE FUN.



RIGHT, BUT MAYBE THE EASTER BUNNY SHOULD HAVE THOUGHT ABOUT ALL THE LAUNDRY MRS. BUNNY WILL HAVE TO DO.

MAYBE HE DID, BUT ALSO MAYBE HE'S NOT AS MUCH OF A NEAT FREAK AS MRS. BUNNY CAN BE SOMETIMES.

"NEAT FREAK," HUH?

4-4

WHEN I WRITE MY AUTOBIOGRAPHY, I THINK I'LL LEAVE THIS PART OUT.

I WOULD.

KIRKMAN & SCOTT

I WANT TO GIVE DAD SOMETHING COOL FOR HIS BIRTHDAY, BUT I DON'T KNOW WHAT.

WELL, CAN YOU THINK OF SOMETHING THAT MAKES HIM HAPPY?
...AND THEN SHE SAID, "THAT LADY AT THE HARDWARE STORE."
SHE JUST TOLD ME A JOKE ABOUT HAMMERS!
©2021, BABY BLUES BROS LLC DIST. BY KING FEATURES SYNDICATE 4-5
KIRKMAN & SCOTT

YOU SHOULD LET ME DRAW A TATTOO ON YOUR BACK AS DAD'S BIRTHDAY SURPRISE.
DO YOU THINK HE'D LIKE IT?
WHAT FATHER WOULDN'T LOVE A FLAMING SKULL INSIDE A BARBED WIRE HEART ON HIS KID'S BACK?
GOOD POINT.
I'LL EVEN USE A PERMANENT MARKER.
YOU'RE SUCH A GOOD SISTER.
©2021, BABY BLUES BROS LLC DIST. BY KING FEATURES SYNDICATE 4-6
KIRKMAN & SCOTT

HOW'S MY "TATTOO" COMING?
ALMOST FINISHED.

THERE! PERFECT!
©2021, BABY BLUES BROS LLC DIST. BY KING FEATURES SYNDICATE 4-7

NOW BE SURE TO SHOW IT TO EVERYBODY ON THE PLAYGROUND TOMORROW.
WILL DO!
Kick Me
KIRKMAN & SCOTT

MOM, CAN I BE UNGROUNDED NOW?
ARE YOU SORRY FOR WHAT YOU DID?

YOU MEAN HANGING A RUBBER SNAKE IN FRONT OF ZOE'S DOOR THAT SCARED HER SO BAD THAT SHE ALMOST WET HER PANTS?
©2021, BABY BLUES BROS LLC DIST. BY KING FEATURES SYNDICATE 4-8
KIRKMAN & SCOTT

YES. EXTREMELY SORRY.
BACK TO YOUR ROOM.

MA?
WREN! WHERE DID YOU GET THOSE SHARP SCISSORS??
ARE YOU OKAY?? DID YOU CUT YOURSELF?
DISASTER AVERTED!
YEAH...UNTIL YOU SEE WHAT USED TO BE THE COUCH.
©2021, BABY BLUES BROS LLC DIST. BY KING FEATURES SYNDICATE 4-9
KIRKMAN & SCOTT

IF YOU'RE LOOKING FOR THE KIDS, THEY'RE IN ZOE'S ROOM PLAYING MONOPOLY.
REALLY? THAT'S A PRETTY SOPHISTICATED GAME FOR-
GET MY HOTEL OUT OF YOUR NOSE!
THEN QUIT PRETENDING YOUR DOG IS PEEING ON MY RACE CAR!
OH.
©2021, BABY BLUES BROS LLC DIST. BY KING FEATURES SYNDICATE 4-10
KIRKMAN & SCOTT

WHEN THE KIDS WENT TO SCHOOL EVERY DAY, IT WAS CHAOS IN THE MORNINGS, BUT NOW...

...IT'S WORSE.
HEY!
GAAH! MY REPORT!
KIDS! YOU GO "LIVE" IN TEN SECONDS!
©2021, BABY BLUES BROS LLC DIST. BY KING FEATURES SYNDICATE 4-12
KIRKMAN & SCOTT

HI. WHAT DID YOU DO TODAY?
PLANTED FLOWERS IN THE POTS BY THE FRONT PORCH.

REALLY? I DIDN'T NOTICE.
THAT'S BECAUSE WREN NOTICED THEM FIRST.
FOWERS!
KIRKMAN & SCOTT
©2021, BABY BLUES BROS LLC DIST. BY KING FEATURES SYNDICATE 4-13

WREN! LUNCHTIME!

SHAKE! SHAKE! SHAKE!
4-11

MUNCH!
MUNCH!

CRUNCH!
CRUNCH!
CRUNCH!

WREN! LUNCHTIME!
KIRKMAN & SCOTT

SIGH!
HOW DID I RAISE SUCH A PICKY EATER?

URRRRGGH!
©2021, BABY BLUES BROS LLC DIST. BY KING FEATURES SYNDICATE 4-14

PRE-PANDEMIC JEANS, MEET POST-PANDEMIC HIPS.

I HAVE TO START EXERCISING MORE!
LOOK AT ME!
©2021, BABY BLUES BROS LLC DIST. BY KING FEATURES SYNDICATE 4-15
WE'VE GOTTEN WAY TOO FAT.
THAT WENT FROM "ME" TO "WE" AWFULLY FAST.

MAYBE WE COULD LOSE SOME WEIGHT IF WE STARTED TAKING WALKS AFTER DINNER.
LET'S TRY IT.

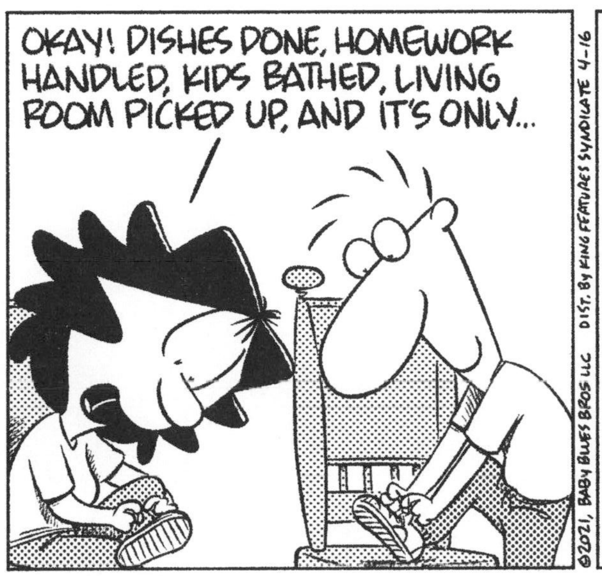
OKAY! DISHES DONE, HOMEWORK HANDLED, KIDS BATHED, LIVING ROOM PICKED UP, AND IT'S ONLY...
©2021, BABY BLUES BROS LLC DIST. BY KING FEATURES SYNDICATE 4-16

...MIDNIGHT.
KIRKMAN & SCOTT

YAHH!
SMASH!
KICK!
CHOP!
PUNCH!

YAWN.
KIRKMAN & SCOTT
©2021, BABY BLUES BROS LLC DIST. BY KING FEATURES SYNDICATE 4-17

ZOE WON'T SCREAM AT ME!

PING!
FOOMP!
OOF!
PING!
PING!
SPANG!
GAH!
PING!
CONK!
OW!
TIME OUT!
GOOD THING YOU WORE A HELMET.
WHEN DID YOU GET SO GOOD?
©2021, BABY BLUES BROS LLC DIST. BY KING FEATURES SYNDICATE 4-18
KIRKMAN & SCOTT

LOOKS LIKE A LIGHTBULB BURNED OUT.
POP!
WHAT DO YOU MEAN?

IT DIED. KAPUT. IT'S NO GOOD ANYMORE.
KIRKMAN & SCOTT
©2021, BABY BLUES BROS LLC DIST. BY KING FEATURES SYNDICATE 4-19

SO, ARE WE MOVING?

ALL YOU DO IS UNSCREW THE OLD BULB, AND SCREW IN A NEW ONE.
CAN I DO IT?

TURN IT THAT WAY...
...NO. THE OTHER—
URGH! NEVER MIND.
©2021, BABY BLUES BROS LLC DIST. BY KING FEATURES SYNDICATE 4-20

DON'T MENTION THIS TO YOUR MOTHER.
YEAH. SHE'D THINK YOUR DAD IS NUTS.
KIRKMAN & SCOTT

♫ GUESS WHAT I ♪ JUST DI-I-I-D...

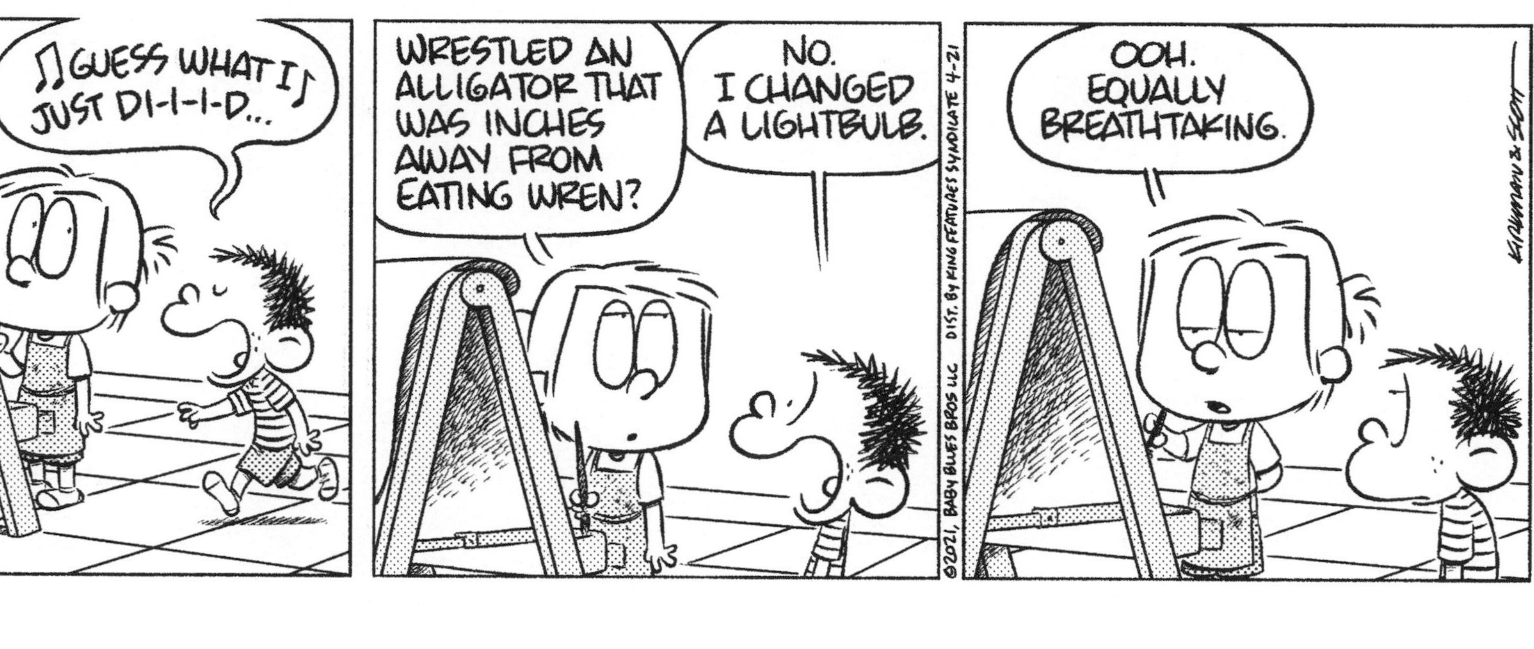
WRESTLED AN ALLIGATOR THAT WAS INCHES AWAY FROM EATING WREN?
NO. I CHANGED A LIGHTBULB.
OOH. EQUALLY BREATHTAKING.
©2021, BABY BLUES BROS LLC DIST. BY KING FEATURES SYNDICATE 4-21
KIRKMAN & SCOTT

HOW COME HAMMIE GOT TO CHANGE A LIGHTBULB AND I DIDN'T?
BECAUSE HE WAS THERE WHEN IT BURNED OUT, AND HE WANTED TO HELP.
I WANT TO DO SOMETHING BORING, TOO!
AM I REALLY HAVING THIS CONVERSATION?
©2021, BABY BLUES BROS LLC DIST. BY KING FEATURES SYNDICATE 4-22
KIRKMAN & SCOTT

YOU LOVE HAMMIE MORE THAN YOU LOVE ME!
NO, I DON'T.

ALL HE DID WAS SCREW A LIGHTBULB INTO A SOCKET!
WAAAA! THAT PROVES IT! YOU HATE ME!

YOU WANT TO HELP ME OUT A LITTLE HERE?
YOU'RE THE MONSTER. YOU FIGURE IT OUT.

OKAY, FROM NOW ON, ANY LIFE SKILLS I PASS ALONG WILL INVOLVE ALL OF YOU.
OKAY.
GOOD.

TODAY'S LESSON IS TOILET SCRUBBING!

CLASS DISMISSED, I GUESS.
NICE TRY.
ZIP!
ZIP!

MAY I TAKE
YOUR ORDER?

OKAY. WE'RE GOING TO DO THIS IN AN ORDERLY FASHION, ONE AT A TIME.
MAY I TAKE YOUR ORDER?
NUGGETS!
NO! TATER TOTS!
CHEESE-BURGER!
SUNDAE!
HOT DOG!
FRIES!
HOT DOG!
HOT DOG!
MILKSHAKE!
4-25
WHAT DID I JUST SAY??
OH, HI MISTER MacPHERSON.
KIRKMAN & SCOTT

SEE, WREN? THIS IS YOU WHEN YOU WERE A BABY.
PHOTOS

AND THIS IS YOU NOW.
PHOTOS
KIRKMAN & SCOTT
©2021, BABY BLUES BROS LLC DIST. BY KING FEATURES SYNDICATE 4-26

THE DIFFERENCES WILL BE MORE STARTLING WHEN YOU GET TO BE MY AGE.

HEY, EVERYBODY! DAD'S GOING TO PLAY A SONG!
PLINK! PLINNNNK!

I APPRECIATE THE ENTHUSIASM, BUT I'M REALLY NOT THAT GOOD YET.
©2021, BABY BLUES BROS LLC DIST. BY KING FEATURES SYNDICATE 4-27

WE KNOW.
I'M JUST HERE FOR THE BAD WORDS.
KIRKMAN & SCOTT

WHAT'S THIS?
THE NEIGHBORS' LAWN GNOMES. I CALL THEM LANCE AND ANDY.

WHY ARE THEY HERE?
THEY LOOKED LONELY, SO I ADOPTED THEM.
©2021, BABY BLUES BROS LLC DIST. BY KING FEATURES SYNDICATE 4-28

I'M GETTING OUT OF HERE BEFORE THE FBI GETS INVOLVED.
FBI?? AM I OLD ENOUGH TO HAVE FINGERPRINTS?
KIRKMAN & SCOTT

ZOE! YOU GOTTA HELP ME SNEAK LANCE AND ANDY BACK TO THEIR HOME BEFORE THEIR OWNERS MISS THEM!
HOW?
WE'LL DRESS LIKE NINJAS AND SNEAK THEM BACK TONIGHT UNDER COVER OF DARKNESS.
YEAH!
©2021, BABY BLUES BROS LLC DIST. BY KING FEATURES SYNDICATE 4-29

I DON'T HAVE ANY NINJA CLOTHES, SO I'LL WEAR MY LIGHT-UP SHIRT WITH SEQUINS.
WHY DON'T YOU JUST HIRE A MARCHING BAND WHILE YOU'RE AT IT?
KIRKMAN & SCOTT

LET'S DO THIS
JUST A SEC.

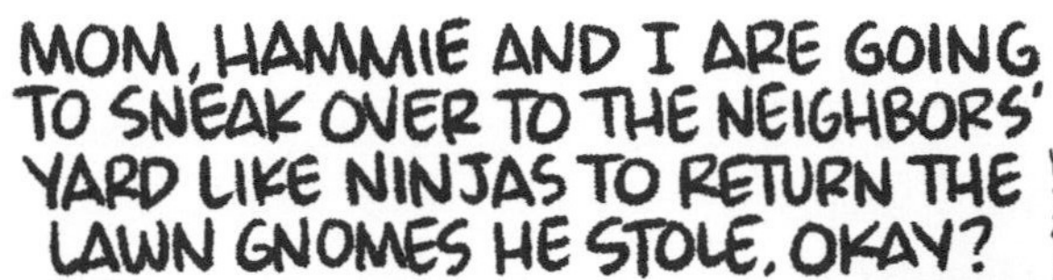
MOM, HAMMIE AND I ARE GOING TO SNEAK OVER TO THE NEIGHBORS' YARD LIKE NINJAS TO RETURN THE LAWN GNOMES HE STOLE, OKAY?

©2021, BABY BLUES BROS LLC DIST. BY KING FEATURES SYNDICATE

THAT FELT GOOD. LET'S GO.
KIRKMAN & SCOTT 4-30

STOP WORRYING. WE'RE JUST RETURNING A COUPLE OF LAWN GNOMES!
IF THE FBI CATCHES US, WE'RE GOING TO JAIL!

IF THE NEIGHBORS CATCH US, WE'RE GOING TO JAIL!
IF MOM AND DAD CATCH US...
KIRKMAN & SCOTT
©2021, BABY BLUES BROS LLC DIST. BY KING FEATURES SYNDICATE 5-1

...IT'LL BE WAY, WAY WORSE.
I CAN'T DO SOLITARY CONFINEMENT! I HAVE TO CHAT!

DINK! DINK!
DINK-A-DINK!

BE MY GUEST.
~PLOP!
GO AHEAD... MAKE MY DAY.
DINK! DINK! DINK-A-DINK!
YOU'RE BLUFFING.
©2021, BABY BLUES BROS LLC DIST. BY KING FEATURES SYNDICATE
SPLUT
AAUGH!
IF I WERE YOU, I'D TRY REVERSING THE REVERSE PSYCHOLOGY.
KIRKMAN & SCOTT 5-2

WHAT WOULD YOU LIKE FOR MOTHER'S DAY?
OH, GOSH...

AFTER THE PAST YEAR, I'D BE HAPPY WITH ANYTHING THAT'S NOT A VIRUS.

©2021, BABY BLUES BROS LLC DIST. BY KING FEATURES SYNDICATE 5-3
YOU'RE BUYING MOM AN AIR COMPRESSOR??
SHE SAID IT WOULD MAKE HER HAPPY.
KIRKMAN & SCOTT

THE KIDS WANT TO MAKE YOU BREAKFAST ON SUNDAY.
THAT'S SWEET!

I'M NOT SURE WHAT THEY'RE PLANNING TO MAKE.
KIRKMAN & SCOTT

©2021, BABY BLUES BROS LLC DIST. BY KING FEATURES SYNDICATE 5-4
ANY REQUESTS?
HOLD THE PLAY-DOH.

I FINISHED MOM'S MOTHER'S DAY CARD.
WHAT'S IT SAY?
I ♡ HEART U, AND HAMMIE IS FLICKING BOOGERS AT ME.
I REALLY LIKE THE BOOGER PART.
WELL, THAT'S THE CRUX OF THE MESSAGE.
©2021, BABY BLUES BROS LLC DIST. BY KING FEATURES SYNDICATE 5-5
KIRKMAN & SCOTT
SO, THERE'S SANTA AND HIS REINDEER, AND RUDOLPH HAS A...
...FLASHLIGHT?
FLAMETHROWER.
INTERESTING MOTHER'S DAY CARD.
SHE WON'T GET ANOTHER ONE LIKE IT.
©2021, BABY BLUES BROS LLC DIST. BY KING FEATURES SYNDICATE 5-6
KIRKMAN & SCOTT

WREN MADE A MOTHER'S DAY CARD FOR MOM!
AWWW.

THOSE ARE HER HANDPRINTS.
VERY NICE.
MOM
©2021, BABY BLUES BROS LLC DIST. BY KING FEATURES SYNDICATE 5-7

YEAH, THAT'S THE GOOD NEWS...
MOM
KIRKMAN & SCOTT

CAREFUL... CAREFUL...

CRINKLE
GASP!
©2021, BABY BLUES BROS LLC DIST. BY KING FEATURES SYNDICATE 5-8

YOU TRIPPED THE CANDY-PAPER ALARM!
STEP AWAY FROM THE MOTHER'S DAY GIFT!
KIRKMAN & SCOTT

I'LL TAKE THE KIDS FOR A LITTLE HIKE SO YOU CAN GET SOME "WANDA TIME."

THAT'S SWEET.

HAPPY MOTHER'S DAY

MOM

I WONDER IF DARRYL PACKED WATER AND SUNSCREEN?

©2021, BABY BLUES BROS LLC DIST. BY KING FEATURES SYNDICATE

OR SNACKS? WREN IS A BEAST WHEN HER BLOOD SUGAR IS LOW.

DID HE EVEN BRING THEIR JACKETS?

WHAT ABOUT SNAKES?

AND TICKS?

IF DARRYL'S PHONE DIES...

...HOW WILL THE SEARCH PARTIES KNOW WHERE TO LOOK??

KIRKMAN & SCOTT 5-9

WE'RE HOME!

ENJOY YOUR AFTERNOON?

HOW COULD I? YOU HAD ME WORRIED SICK!

AHA! I CAUGHT YOU RESEARCHING COOL FAMILY VACATIONS, DIDN'T I?

YES, BUT IT'S A SURPRISE. DON'T LOOK!
©2021, BABY BLUES BROS LLC DIST. BY KING FEATURES SYNDICATE 5-10

LIAR.
ORDERING A KNEE BRACE SOUNDED LAME.
KIRKMAN & SCOTT

DAD, THERE'S A RUMOR THAT YOU'RE TAKING US ON A MONTH-LONG TOUR OF THEME PARKS THIS SUMMER.

WHERE IN THE WORLD DID YOU HEAR A RUMOR LIKE THAT?
©2021, BABY BLUES BROS LLC DIST. BY KING FEATURES SYNDICATE 5-11

I STARTED IT, BUT IT'S REALLY GAINING SUPPORT WITH THE PUBLIC.
I'LL BET IT IS.
KIRKMAN & SCOTT

BEFORE YOU SAY ANYTHING, JUST HEAR ME OUT.
WE COULD RENT A MOTORHOME FOR OUR SUMMER VACATION!
THE KIDS WOULD LIKE THAT.
THIRTY-FOOT DIESEL PUSHER ROARING DOWN THE HIGHWAY, ANSWERING THE CALL OF THE OPEN ROAD...
THIS IS FOR THE KIDS, RIGHT?
KIRKMAN & SCOTT
©2021, BABY BLUES BROS LLC DIST. BY KING FEATURES SYNDICATE 5-12

GUYS, I HAVE AN IDEA.
WE'RE THINKING ABOUT US RENTING A MOTORHOME FOR OUR SUMMER VACATION.
I EXPECTED MORE EXCITEMENT.
WHO ARE YOU AND WHAT HAVE YOU DONE WITH OUR UN-FUN DAD?
KIRKMAN & SCOTT
©2021, BABY BLUES BROS LLC DIST. BY KING FEATURES SYNDICATE 5-13

SOME OF THESE MOTORHOMES ARE BIG AND LUXURIOUS BUT SUPER-EXPENSIVE.
THAT ONE HAS A SIXTY-INCH FLATSCREEN.

BUT SOME OF THESE SMALLER, SIMPLER ONES ARE JUST AS GOOD, RIGHT?
KIRKMAN & SCOTT
©2021, BABY BLUES BROS LLC DIST. BY KING FEATURES SYNDICATE 5-14
...RIGHT?
I DIDN'T THINK WE'D HEAR CRICKETS UNTIL WE SET UP CAMP.

I THINK WE CAN AFFORD TO RENT THIS MOTORHOME, BUT IT'S PRETTY SMALL.
COZY CAN BE GOOD!

TOOT!
©2021, BABY BLUES BROS LLC DIST. BY KING FEATURES SYNDICATE 5-15
KIRKMAN & SCOTT

MOVING ON TO THE LARGER MODELS...
ONE WITH EXTRA WINDOWS!

HA! HA! HA! HA!

LOOK AT THESE!
HA! HA! YOU SHOULD BUY THEM FOR DAD!

HA! HA! HA! HA! HA! HA! HA! HA!
HA! HA! HA! HA!

HEY DAD... WE BOUGHT YOU THESE!
COOL.
5-16

COME ON, HAMMIE! I'LL GIVE YOU A RIDE TO PRACTICE!
GASP!
©2021, BABY BLUES BROS LLC DIST. BY KING FEATURES SYNDICATE

NEVER GIVE A MAN A JOKE GIFT.
ESPECIALLY IF IT'S CLOTHES.

HEY, KIDS! HERE COMES DADDY IN THE MOTORHOME WE RENTED!

CRUNCH!
©2021, BABY BLUES BROS LLC DIST. BY KING FEATURES SYNDICATE 5-17
AND THERE HE GOES TO BUY US A NEW MAILBOX.
GET AN ARMORED ONE, DAD!
KIRKMAN & SCOTT

DARRYL, THIS MOTORHOME IS HUGE!
YEAH, IT'S A LITTLE BIGGER THAN I EXPECTED, TOO.

WE'LL BE FINE AS SOON AS I GET THE HANG OF IT.
©2021, BABY BLUES BROS LLC DIST. BY KING FEATURES SYNDICATE 5-18

I JUST HOPE YOUR LEARNING CURVE HAS A GUARDRAIL.
KIRKMAN & SCOTT

WOW! THESE CHAIRS SPIN AROUND! WATCH!

WHOOSH!WH
KIRKMAN & SCOTT

BARF!
UH-OH.
AND WE'RE NOT EVEN OUT OF THE DRIVEWAY YET.
©2021, BABY BLUES BROS LLC DIST. BY KING FEATURES SYNDICATE 5-19

LOOK OUT, AMERICA! THE MacPHERSONS ARE ABOUT TO HIT THE ROAD!
DARRYL?
YEAH, SWEETIE?
WHERE ARE WE GOING EXACTLY?
I KNEW WE MISSED A DETAIL.
THERE GOES ANOTHER MAILBOX, DAD!
CRUNCH!
KIRKMAN & SCOTT
©2021, BABY BLUES BROS LLC DIST. BY KING FEATURES SYNDICATE 5-20

I HAVE AN IDEA!

LET'S DRIVE THE MOTORHOME TO THE OCEAN!
YAY! COOL!
©2021, BABY BLUES BROS LLC DIST. BY KING FEATURES SYNDICATE 5-21

WHICH OCEAN?
THE ONE THAT INVOLVES THE LEAST AMOUNT OF TURNING.
KIRKMAN & SCOTT

MOM, I NEED TO USE THE RESTROOM. CAN WE STOP?

ZOE, THE MOTORHOME HAS A BATHROOM, REMEMBER?
YEAH, BUT...
©2021, BABY BLUES BROS LLC DIST. BY KING FEATURES SYNDICATE 5-22
KIRKMAN & SCOTT

...I DON'T WANT TO GET BUCKED OFF THE SEAT AGAIN.
THAT WAS A POTHOLE! NOT MY FAULT!

OOPS!
SPLOOSH!
KIRKMAN & SCOTT
SHOULD WE MOP THAT UP?
HERE, USE THIS QUILT.
5-23
©2021, BABY BLUES BROS LLC DIST. BY KING FEATURES SYNDICATE

DRIP!
DON'T TELL!
DRIP!
DRIP!
UM, I DON'T THINK I'LL HAVE TO.
UM, THAT LOOKS EVEN WORSE.
MOM WANTS NEW CARPET, ANYWAY, RIGHT?
I CAN PRETEND TO BE ASLEEP LONGER THAN YOU CAN.
YOU'RE ON.

©2021, BABY BLUES BROS LLC DIST. BY KING FEATURES SYNDICATE 5-24
KIRKMAN & SCOTT
WHAT TIME IS DINNER?
CAN I HAVE A SANDWICH?
I WANT CHIPS!
GREAT VACATION, RIGHT, SWEETIE?
CHIPS

OKAY, HAMMIE, YOU SLEEP HERE, ZOE, YOU'RE HERE...
...AND WREN WILL BE...
SHE'S NOT SLEEPING IN SINK!
WE HAVE MORE KIDS THAN MOTORHOME.
KIRKMAN & SCOTT
©2021, BABY BLUES BROS LLC DIST. BY KING FEATURES SYNDICATE 5-25

HERE'S SOME COFFEE...
THANK YOU.
KIRKMAN & SCOTT

...AND YOUR LOTTERY NUMBER.
FOR WHAT?
©2021, BABY BLUES BROS LLC DIST. BY KING FEATURES SYNDICATE 5-26

FIVE PEOPLE, ONE BATHROOM, REMEMBER?
CAN WE PLEASE START THE DRAWING?

WHAT ARE YOU DOING, DAD?
EMPTYING THE HOLDING TANK.

WHAT'S IT BEEN HOLDING?
©2021, BABY BLUES BROS LLC DIST. BY KING FEATURES SYNDICATE 5-27

OH, A LITTLE OF THIS AND A LITTLE OF THAT...
YOU KNOW WHAT IT SMELLS LIKE, RIGHT?
KIRKMAN & SCOTT

THERE IT IS, GUYS! THE PACIFIC OCEAN!
LAST ONE IN IS A ROTTEN EGG!
YEEP! GAH! YIPES! EEEEEEK!
THE WATER LOOKS WARMER IN THE MOVIES.
KIRKMAN & SCOTT
©2021, BABY BLUES BROS LLC DIST. BY KING FEATURES SYNDICATE 5-28

RENTING THE MOTORHOME WAS A GREAT IDEA, DARRYL.
THANKS.
THIS WHOLE TRIP HAS BEEN PRACTICALLY PERFECT.
WHICH, FOR US, SHOULD BE A WARNING SIGN.
IT'S A LONG DRIVE BACK. PLENTY OF TIME LEFT FOR DISASTERS.
KIRKMAN & SCOTT
©2021, BABY BLUES BROS LLC DIST. BY KING FEATURES SYNDICATE 5-29

POP! POP!
POP! POP!
POP!

WAAAAA!
MOM! WREN TOYED HERSELF INTO A CORNER AGAIN!
KIRKMAN & SCOTT
©2021, BABY BLUES BROS LLC DIST. BY KING FEATURES SYNDICATE 5-30

WASN'T HAMMIE'S CHECKUP TODAY?
YEP. THE DOCTOR SAID EVERYTHING IS GOOD.
HM.
SO, HE'S GONNA STAY LIKE THIS?
APPARENTLY.
©2021, BABY BLUES BROS LLC DIST. BY KING FEATURES SYNDICATE 5-31
KIRKMAN & SCOTT

SO, NO CONCERNS AT ALL FROM HAMMIE'S DOCTOR?
WELL, SHE DID SAY HE WAS A LITTLE SHORT FOR HIS AGE.
WHAT???
BUT HIS HEARING IS EXCELLENT.
©2021, BABY BLUES BROS LLC DIST. BY KING FEATURES SYNDICATE 6-1
KIRKMAN & SCOTT

THE DOCTOR SAID THAT I'M TOO SHORT??
HAMMIE, NO.

EVERYONE GROWS AT A DIFFERENT RATE. YOU'RE PERFECTLY NORMAL.
©2021, BABY BLUES BROS LLC DIST. BY KING FEATURES SYNDICATE 6-2

KIRKMAN & SCOTT
FOR SOME REASON, I'M HUNGRY FOR SHRIMP.
NOT HELPFUL, ZOE.

GUYS, THE DOCTOR SAYS I'M TOO SHORT, SO YOU NEED TO STRETCH ME.

WREN, ZOE, GRAB MY FEET AND PULL!
KIRKMAN & SCOTT
©2021, BABY BLUES BROS LLC DIST. BY KING FEATURES SYNDICATE 6-3

WHEN WAS THE LAST TIME THOSE FEET WERE WASHED?
WHAT MONTH IS THIS?

IT STINKS THAT I'M SHORT FOR MY AGE.
HAMMIE...
...I WAS THE SAME WAY, AND LOOK AT ME NOW! TALL, HANDSOME, WILDLY INTELLIGENT...
©2021, BABY BLUES BROS LLC DIST. BY KING FEATURES SYNDICATE 6-4
KIRKMAN & SCOTT
DARRYL...
...AND STRONG! OH MY GOSH! THE STRENGTH!
©2021, BABY BLUES BROS LLC DIST. BY KING FEATURES SYNDICATE 6-5
KIRKMAN & SCOTT
I THINK WREN MIGHT BE CONSTIPATED.
THE QUALITY OF OUR PILLOW TALK HAS SEVERELY DECLINED.

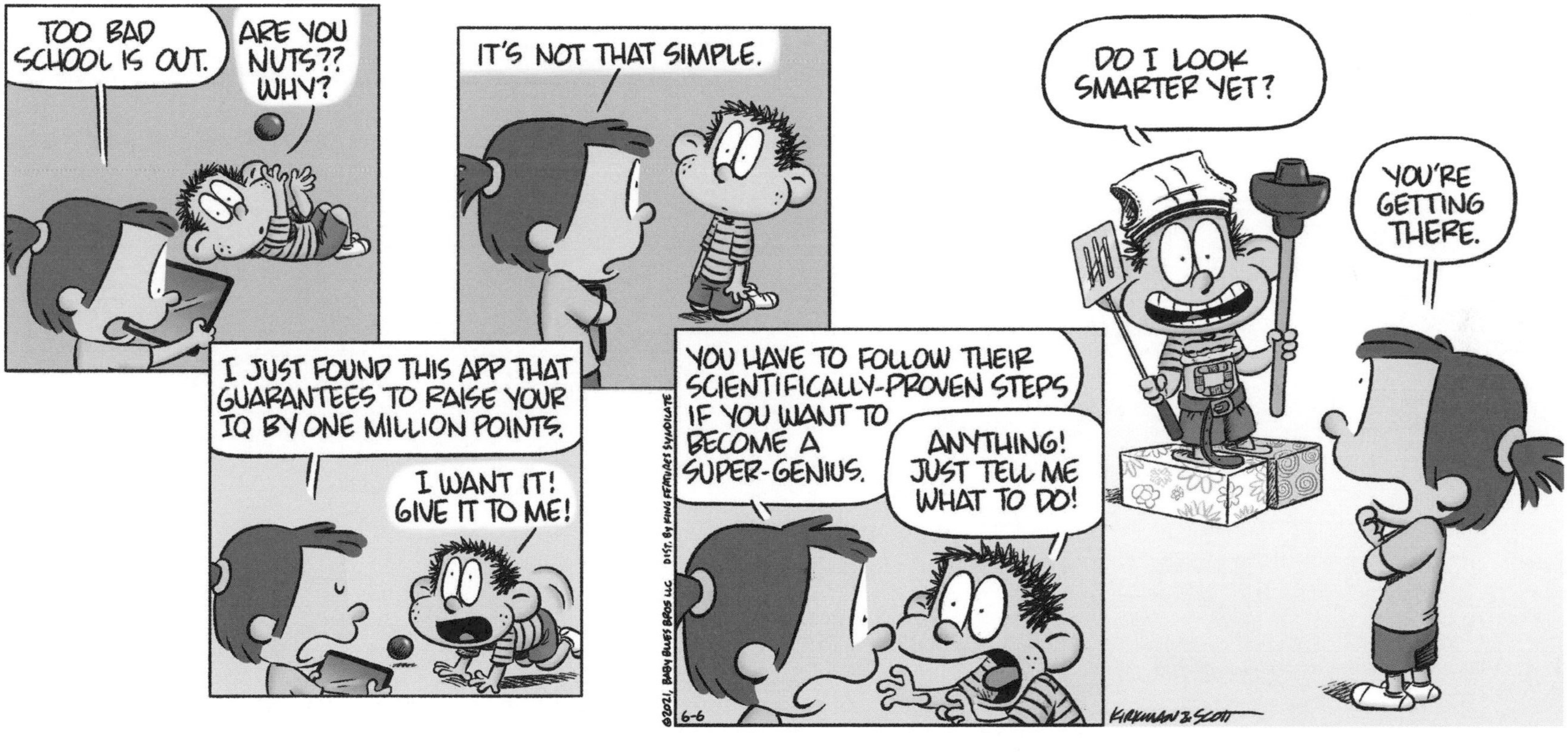

TOO BAD SCHOOL IS OUT.

ARE YOU NUTS?? WHY?

I JUST FOUND THIS APP THAT GUARANTEES TO RAISE YOUR IQ BY ONE MILLION POINTS.

I WANT IT! GIVE IT TO ME!

IT'S NOT THAT SIMPLE.

YOU HAVE TO FOLLOW THEIR SCIENTIFICALLY-PROVEN STEPS IF YOU WANT TO BECOME A SUPER-GENIUS.

ANYTHING! JUST TELL ME WHAT TO DO!

DO I LOOK SMARTER YET?

YOU'RE GETTING THERE.



6-6

KIRKMAN & SCOTT

HOW WAS WORK?
EXHAUSTING. I SPENT ALL DAY DELETING EMAILS.
SOMETIMES I PRETEND I'M A CONSTRUCTION GUY AND MY DELETE KEY IS A SLEDGEHAMMER.
MY BIG, STRONG WORKING MAN.
WANT TO FEEL MY GUNS?
©2021, BABY BLUES BROS LLC DIST. BY KING FEATURES SYNDICATE 6-7
KIRKMAN & SCOTT

OKAY, I'M READY!
ALL THIS TO FIX A LOOSE DRAWER GLIDE?
WELL, IT'S LIKE THEY SAY, WANDA...
...DRESS FOR THE JOB YOU WANT, NOT THE JOB YOU HAVE!
IS THIS A MIDLIFE CRISIS OR JUST TEMPORARY INSANITY?
©2021, BABY BLUES BROS LLC DIST. BY KING FEATURES SYNDICATE 6-8
KIRKMAN & SCOTT

I WAS JUST MESSING WITH YOU, WANDA. I DON'T REALLY WANT TO BECOME A CONSTRUCTION WORKER.
KIRKMAN & SCOTT

I LIKE WORKING WITH MY HANDS, BUT I'M STICKING WITH WHAT I DO BEST.
©2021, BABY BLUES BROS LLC DIST. BY KING FEATURES SYNDICATE 6-9

SITTING ON YOUR BUTT FOR EIGHT HOURS A DAY?
FEAR MY BUNS, CORPORATE AMERICA!
SLAP!

THE BASES ARE LOADED IN THE BOTTOM OF THE NINTH, AND THE CROWD STARTS TO CHANT,
HAM-MIE! HAM-MIE!

AND IT'S A GRAND SLAM!
WHIFF!
©2021, BABY BLUES BROS LLC DIST. BY KING FEATURES SYNDICATE 6-10

REALLY?
IF I CAN IMAGINE THE CROWD, I CAN IMAGINE THE HOMER!
KIRKMAN & SCOTT

THUNK!
DID YOU SEE THAT???

I FLIPPED THE WATER BOTTLE IN THE AIR, AND IT LANDED JUST LIKE THAT!
WOW. GOSH. GOOD FOR YOU.
©2021, BABY BLUES BROS LLC DIST. BY KING FEATURES SYNDICATE 6-11
KIRKMAN & SCOTT
THAT WAS A REAL STROKE OF AVERAGE.

HAMMIE, DID YOU BRUSH YOUR TEETH?
YES*
* BUT NOT VERY WELL.
©2021, BABY BLUES BROS LLC DIST. BY KING FEATURES SYNDICATE 6-12
KIRKMAN & SCOTT
MOM ALWAYS READS THE FINE PRINT.

Zoe
is a

COOKI
Zoe
is a
I DON'T THINK I'M GETTING ENOUGH ATTENTION FROM OUR PARENTS. 
YOU CAN HAVE SOME OF MINE!
6-13
KIRKMAN & SCOTT

WANDA, I JUST FOUND DOG POOP IN THE YARD!
OH.
DID YOU GET RID OF IT?
YES, YES, I DID.
IS THAT ALL YOU NEED ME FOR? BECAUSE I HAVE THINGS TO DO.
A LITTLE SHARED OUTRAGE WOULD BE NICE.
©2021, BABY BLUES BROS LLC DIST. BY KING FEATURES SYNDICATE 6-14
KIRKMAN & SCOTT

AARGH!
NOW THERE'S DOG POOP IN THE **FRONT** YARD!
HAVE I TOLD YOU HOW MUCH I ENJOY THESE LAWN REPORTS?
IT'S A POOPADEMIC!
©2021, BABY BLUES BROS LLC DIST. BY KING FEATURES SYNDICATE 6-15
KIRKMAN & SCOTT

DOG POOP IN OUR YARD IS A BIG DEAL, WANDA.
KIRKMAN & SCOTT

SOME DOG OWNER IS BEING UN-NEIGHBORLY, IRRESPONSIBLE AND DOWNRIGHT RUDE!
©2021, BABY BLUES BROS LLC DIST. BY KING FEATURES SYNDICATE 6-16

IT'S TIME SOMEONE TOOK SOME ACTION!
OH, GOOD. A NEW OBSESSION.

WHAT ARE YOU DOING, DAD?
WAITING.

I'M GOING TO CATCH THE DOG THAT'S BEEN POOPING IN OUR YARD. THIS IS A STAKEOUT.
©2021, BABY BLUES BROS LLC DIST. BY KING FEATURES SYNDICATE 6-17

SOUNDS MORE LIKE A POOP-OUT.
"STAKEOUT" SOUNDS COOLER.
KIRKMAN & SCOTT

AH-HA! THAT'S HIM! THE YARD POOPER!
WOW. HE'S HUGE.
GO AWAY! SHOO!
HE'S NOT LEAVING.
KIRKMAN & SCOTT
©2021, BABY BLUES BROS LLC DIST. BY KING FEATURES SYNDICATE 6-18
AREN'T YOU GOING OUT THERE?
I WANT TO GIVE HIM A PIECE OF MY MIND, NOT A PIECE OF MY LEG.

©2021, BABY BLUES BROS LLC DIST. BY KING FEATURES SYNDICATE 6-19
LOOKS LIKE SOMEBODY MISSED HER DADDY TODAY.
CAN YOU AT LEAST DESCRIBE WHAT'S HAPPENING IN THE GAME?
KIRKMAN & SCOTT

A BAG OF PENCIL ERASERS...
...BACON-SCENTED HAND LOTION...
...A FLY-SHAPED FLY SWATTER...
...MORE PENCIL ERASERS...
...A JAR OF CAPERS...
...SOME CANNED MACKEREL...
...A PREGNANCY TEST KIT...
...A BAG OF CIRCUS PEANUTS CANDY...
...A TUBE OF FUNGAL CREAM AND SOME FAKE UNICORN POOP...

HAPPY FATHER'S DAY!

NEXT YEAR, STEER THE KIDS TO HOME DEPOT INSTEAD OF LETTING THEM LOOSE IN THE DOLLAR STORE.



KIRKMAN & SCOTT 6-20

MOM, CAN I DYE MY HAIR BLUE?
UM, I'LL TALK TO DADDY.
I KNOW WHAT THAT MEANS.
OH? WHAT DOES IT MEAN?
THAT I NEED TO GET TO DADDY FIRST!
GET BACK HERE!!
©2021, BABY BLUES BROS LLC DIST. BY KING FEATURES SYNDICATE 6-21
KIRKMAN & SCOTT

CRASH!
ZIP!
ZIP!
©2021, BABY BLUES BROS LLC DIST. BY KING FEATURES SYNDICATE 6-22
KIRKMAN & SCOTT
IF ANYBODY ASKS, WE ONLY SHOP ON EVEN-NUMBERED AISLES.
CLEANUP ON AISLE FIVE!

A GNAT, A MOSQUITO, A LADYBUG AND A FLY.
KIRKMAN & SCOTT

THAT'S A COOL BUG COLLECTION.
©2021, BABY BLUES BROS LLC DIST. BY KING FEATURES SYNDICATE 6-23

HOW DID YOU CATCH THEM ALL SO FAST?

HA! HA!
HA! HA! THAT'S MY FAVORITE PART!

WE'RE SO MUCH ALIKE THAT SOMETIMES I THINK WE COULD BE TWINS.
©2021, BABY BLUES BROS LLC DIST. BY KING FEATURES SYNDICATE 6-24
KIRKMAN & SCOTT

SHE STARTED IT!

GRASS STAINS, BICYCLE GREASE, CHOCOLATE, KETCHUP, MUSTARD, WATERMELON JUICE AND DIRT.
KIRKMAN & SCOTT
CONGRATULATIONS. THAT'S A WHOLE SUMMER'S WORTH OF STAINS IN ONE DAY.
WHAT DO I WIN?
©2021, BABY BLUES BROS LLC DIST. BY KING FEATURES SYNDICATE 6-25

WHERE DO YOU KEEP THE BOOKS THAT ARE ONLY ONE PAGE OR LESS?
SHHH! QUIET PLEASE
KIRKMAN & SCOTT
©2021, BABY BLUES BROS LLC
DIST. BY KING FEATURES SYNDICATE 6-26
HAMMIE!

STRIKE FOUR! STRIKE FIVE! STRIKE SIX!
WHIFF!
WHIFF!
WHIFF!

WHIFF!

STRIKE ONE!
I WASN'T READY!

STRIKE TWO!
I WASN'T READY!
WHIFF!

STRIKE THREE!
I WASN'T READY!

STRIKE FOUR! STRIKE FIVE! STRIKE SIX!
WHIFF!
WHIFF!
WHIFF!
6-27
©2021, BABY BLUES BROS LLC DIST. BY KING FEATURES SYNDICATE

I THINK IT'S MY TURN TO BAT.
JUST KEEP PITCHING! IF I HIT ONE, I WAS READY!
KIRKMAN & SCOTT

THE ANNUAL COMPANY PICNIC IS SATURDAY!
OH.
YOU MEAN THE PICNIC WHERE YOU ALL TRY TO KILL EACH OTHER IN SILLY COMPETITIONS?
YEAH.
GO TEAM DARRYL.
I KNEW YOU'D BE PUMPED ABOUT IT, TOO!
©2021, BABY BLUES BROS LLC DIST. BY KING FEATURES SYNDICATE 6-28
KIRKMAN & SCOTT

YOU LIKE MY COMPANY'S ANNUAL PICNICS, RIGHT?
©2021, BABY BLUES BROS LLC DIST. BY KING FEATURES SYNDICATE 6-29
YOU AND YOUR CO-WORKERS WILL RUN AROUND LIKE IDIOTS ALL DAY WHILE WE SPOUSES DRINK WINE.
KIRKMAN & SCOTT
YEAH. I'M OKAY WITH THAT.

WHAT'S THIS, DAD?
TRAINING.

MY COMPANY PICNIC IS COMING UP, AND I NEED TO BE IN TIP-TOP SHAPE.
©2021, BABY BLUES BROS LLC DIST. BY KING FEATURES SYNDICATE 6-30

WHAT SHAPE ARE YOU IN NOW?
I'D SAY POTATO-SHAPED.
THIS WORKOUT IS NOW CLOSED TO THE PUBLIC!
KIRKMAN & SCOTT

I MADE THIS UP SO MOM CAN CHEER YOU ON AT THE PICNIC.

DADDY! DADDY! TRIES HIS BEST, WAY BEHIND ALL THE REST!
©2021, BABY BLUES BROS LLC DIST. BY KING FEATURES SYNDICATE 7-1

BECAUSE YOU USUALLY LOSE.
YEAH. I GOT THAT PART.
KIRKMAN & SCOTT

WREN, DADDY'S COMPANY PICNIC IS COMING UP, SO HE'S GOING TO BE ACTING WEIRD FOR THE NEXT FEW DAYS.
HE WILL ACTUALLY START BELIEVING THAT HE CAN WIN EVERY ATHLETIC EVENT.
THAT'S NOT TRUE!
FIRST, HE'LL ENTER A STAGE OF DENIAL...
7-2
©2021, BABY BLUES BROS LLC DIST. BY KING FEATURES SYNDICATE
KIRKMAN & SCOTT

MOM AND DAD ARE ARGUING ABOUT THE COMPANY PICNIC.
OOH! COOL!
DAD WANTS HER TO COMPETE IN THE POTATO-SACK RACE, BUT SHE'D RATHER JUST SIT AND RELAX.
IF YOU LISTEN CLOSELY, YOU MIGHT HEAR HER USE HER HBO WORDS...
ARE YOU OUT OF YOUR D–
7-3
©2021, BABY BLUES BROS LLC DIST. BY KING FEATURES SYNDICATE
KIRKMAN & SCOTT

TUG! TUG!

WAP! WAP! WAP!

KICK! KICK! KICK!

SHAKE! SHAKE! SHAKE!

7-4

ARE WE GOING TO WAR?

YOU TRY PUTTING MAKEUP ON WITH AN IMPATIENT TODDLER!

KIRKMAN & SCOTT

BOO!
PRIVATE COLLEGE TUITION.
AAAGH!
IF YOU REALLY WANT TO SCARE HIM, YOU NEED TO GET INSIDE HIS HEAD.
DON'T **DO** THAT!
©2021, BABY BLUES BROS LLC DIST. BY KING FEATURES SYNDICATE 7-5
KIRKMAN & SCOTT

WHAT'S THAT SUPPOSED TO BE?

HEY! NICE AIRPLANE!
©2021, BABY BLUES BROS LLC DIST. BY KING FEATURES SYNDICATE 7-6

IT'S OBVIOUSLY AN AIRPLANE.
KIRKMAN & SCOTT

SQUEEEK!

OH.
IT'S DAD.
©2021, BABY BLUES BROS LLC DIST. BY KING FEATURES SYNDICATE 7-7

THANKS. IT'S GREAT TO SEE YOU TOO!
YOUR CAR'S BRAKES SOUND JUST LIKE THE UPS VAN.
KIRKMAN & SCOTT

WHAT DO YOU WANT TO BE WHEN YOU GROW UP?
ROOFER... TEST PILOT... SOMETHING LIKE THAT.

WHEN I GROW UP, I WANT TO BE JUST LIKE MOM.
©2021, BABY BLUES BROS LLC DIST. BY KING FEATURES SYNDICATE 7-8

BUT WITHOUT ALL THE ANNOYING PARTS.
KIRKMAN & SCOTT

HOO! HAW! YARRRGH!

OKAY, FORGET FORGIVENESS. HOW ABOUT A SIMPLE BLANKET PARDON?

WE'LL DISCUSS THIS WHEN YOUR FATHER GETS HOME.

WHAT THE–?

AAAAUGHHH!

IS HAMMIE ALL RIGHT?

YEAH. HE'S FINE.

OOGH! OOGH! OOGH!

HE DOESN'T LOOK FINE.

I DARED HIM TO EAT A JALAPEÑO PEPPER.

I'LL GO GET HIM SOME MILK.

DON'T BOTHER...

HOO! HOO! HOO!

KIRKMAN & SCOTT



...THAT WAS JUST A REHEARSAL.

OKAY, I'M READY.

7-11

CAN I BE THE FIRST ONE TO SIGN YOUR CAST?

WHAT CAST?
I'M JUST PLANNING AHEAD.
©2021, BABY BLUES BROS LLC DIST. BY KING FEATURES SYNDICATE 7-12
KIRKMAN & SCOTT

DAD, CAN WE HAVE FIVE DOLLARS?
AGAIN??

DO YOU GUYS THINK I'M MADE OF MONEY?
AND JELLY DONUTS.
NOT HELPING.
©2021, BABY BLUES BROS LLC DIST. BY KING FEATURES SYNDICATE 7-13
KIRKMAN & SCOTT

HERE YOU GO, GUYS.
WHAT'S THIS?

LOAN APPLICATIONS. FROM NOW ON, I WANT YOU TO FILL OUT ONE OF THESE BEFORE YOU ASK FOR MONEY.
KIRKMAN & SCOTT

©2021, BABY BLUES BROS LLC DIST. BY KING FEATURES SYNDICATE 7-14
CHARACTER REFERENCES??
ANYONE BUT HAMMIE WILL WORK.

YOU FILLING OUT ONE OF DAD'S LOAN APPLICATIONS?
YEAH. I NEED SOME NEW HOT WHEELS CARS.

YOU CAN'T JUST SAY THAT! IT HAS TO SOUND MORE URGENT AND OFFICIAL, LIKE...
©2021, BABY BLUES BROS LLC DIST. BY KING FEATURES SYNDICATE 7-15

AUTOMOTIVE NEEDS?
IF THAT'S WHAT IT SAYS.
KIRKMAN & SCOTT

DAD, WE DON'T WANT TO FILL OUT LOAN APPLICATIONS ANYMORE.
OKAY.

WE'LL SWITCH TO A MERIT-BASED ALLOWANCE SYSTEM.

©2021, BABY BLUES BROS LLC DIST. BY KING FEATURES SYNDICATE 7-16
KIRKMAN & SCOTT
I'M NOT SURE I LIKE THE SOUND OF THAT.
I WOULDN'T LIKE IT EVEN IF I COULD UNDERSTAND IT.

HAMMIE'S COMING UP TO BAT! LET'S SHOW HIM SOME SUPPORT.

C'MON, HAMMIE!

©2021, BABY BLUES BROS LLC DIST. BY KING FEATURES SYNDICATE 7-17
KIRKMAN & SCOTT
EXCEED OUR SUPER-LOW EXPECTATIONS!
NOT WHAT I HAD IN MIND.

SOME GUY ON TV JUST BOILED YOUR WHOLE VOCABULARY DOWN TO ONE WORD.

CHEETAH! UMGAWA!
WHAT ARE YOU WATCHING?
IT'S AN OLD BLACK AND WHITE TARZAN MOVIE.
UMGAWA! UMGAWA!
WHAT'S "UMGAWA" MEAN?
I'M PRETTY SURE IT'S AN ORDER.
IT PROBABLY MEANS "DO WHAT I SAY," OR "LISTEN TO ME," OR "SCRAM."
SOME GUY ON TV JUST BOILED YOUR WHOLE VOCABULARY DOWN TO ONE WORD.
KIRKMAN & SCOTT
©2021, BABY BLUES BROS LLC DIST. BY KING FEATURES SYNDICATE
7-18

WAIT TILL YOUR DAD GETS HOME, YOUNG MAN!
WILL HE BE HOME BY THREE?

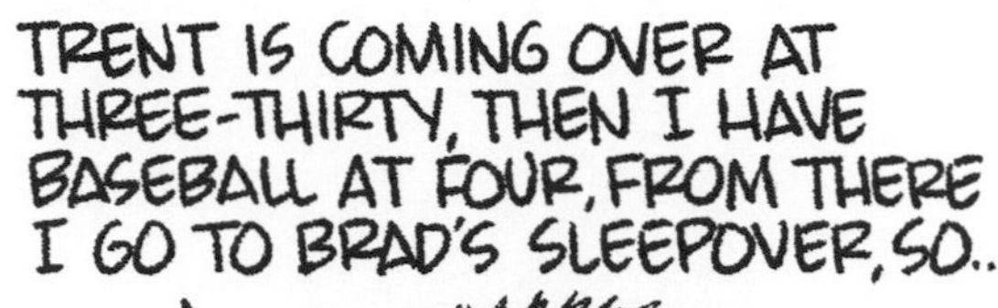
TRENT IS COMING OVER AT THREE-THIRTY, THEN I HAVE BASEBALL AT FOUR, FROM THERE I GO TO BRAD'S SLEEPOVER, SO...

HI, HONEY. WHAT'S UP?
DO YOU HAVE TIME TO SCOLD HAMMIE RIGHT NOW?
OR I COULD WORK HIM IN ON FRIDAY...
KIRKMAN & SCOTT
©2021, BABY BLUES BROS LLC DIST. BY KING FEATURES SYNDICATE 8-2

WHAT'S WREN DOING?
IT'S HER NEW THING.

SHE RUNS IN CIRCLES UNTIL SHE GETS DIZZY AND COLLAPSES.
©2021, BABY BLUES BROS LLC DIST. BY KING FEATURES SYNDICATE 8-3

WHY?
MAYBE SHE'S PRACTICING TO BE A MOM.
KIRKMAN & SCOTT

I LOVE YOU, BARBIE.®
I LOVE YOU, SPIDER-MAN.
WHAT'S GOING ON HERE?

KISS! KISS! KISS!
NO! NO! MOM!

STOP TORMENTING HIM.
WHO ARE WE TO STAND IN THE WAY OF TRUE LOVE?
STOP!

ZOE SAYS MY SPIDER-MAN LOVES HER BARBIE.®
DOES HE?

HECK NO! HE'S A SUPERHERO! HE DOESN'T HAVE TIME!

WHAT ARE YOU DOING?
SETTING A REMINDER TO HAVE THIS CONVERSATION IN TEN YEARS.

I HAVE SOME BAD NEWS.
ABOUT WHAT?

BARBIE® AND SPIDER-MAN BROKE UP.
ARE YOU KIDDING? THAT'S GREAT NEWS!
SHE DUMPED HIM TO MARRY THOR!
NOOOOOO!
KIRKMAN & SCOTT
©2021, BABY BLUES BROS LLC DIST. BY KING FEATURES SYNDICATE 8-6

HI, HAMMIE. WHERE HAVE YOU BEEN?
READING. I FINALLY FOUND A GOOD BOOK.
WHAT'S IT ABOUT?
ALL KINDS OF STUFF. SUPERHEROES, VIDEO GAMES, CARS, YOU NAME IT.
THAT'S A TOY CATALOG!
YEAH. I CAN'T PUT IT DOWN.
KIRKMAN & SCOTT
©2021, BABY BLUES BROS LLC DIST. BY KING FEATURES SYNDICATE 8-7

©2021, BABY BLUES BROS LLC DIST. BY KING FEATURES SYNDICATE
"NAUGHTY" IS A TRIGGER WORD...
I CALL IT "EXPLORING ALTERNATIVE BEHAVIORS."
KIRKMAN & SCOTT 7-25

I'M HOME!
YAY! IT'S DADDY!
HI!

OH. SO YOU'RE THE "FUN" PARENT, AND I'M THE MEAN OLD MOM?
IF THE SHOE FITS...
©2021, BABY BLUES BROS LLC DIST. BY KING FEATURES SYNDICATE 8-9

NOT WHAT I MEANT.
KIRKMAN & SCOTT

HEY, SWEETIE, WHATCHA DOING?

I'M STRUCTURING A HIGH-LEVEL OUTLINE OF CONTENT TO INSERT INTO THE NEWSPAPER TEMPLATE I DESIGNED.
©2021, BABY BLUES BROS LLC DIST. BY KING FEATURES SYNDICATE 8-10
KIRKMAN & SCOTT

I WAS JUST WATCHING CARTOONS AT YOUR AGE.
AND I'M SURE YOU WERE GOOD AT IT.

WHAT ARE YOU DOING?
CREATING A NEWSPAPER.

I'M GOING TO WRITE DOWN ALL THE STUFF THAT GOES ON IN OUR FAMILY.
©2021, BABY BLUES BROS LLC DIST. BY KING FEATURES SYNDICATE 8-11

MY BRAIN KEEPS WORKING DURING THE SUMMER.
I GIVE MINE THREE MONTHS OFF.
KIRKMAN & SCOTT

HERE YOU GO! HOT OFF THE PRINTER!
IS THIS YOUR FAMILY NEWSPAPER?

YEP! I'M THE PUBLISHER OF THE MacPHERSON TIMES!
WELL, LET'S HAVE A LOOK!
©2021, BABY BLUES BROS LLC DIST. BY KING FEATURES SYNDICATE 8-12

PUBLISHER AND PAYWALL.
OH.
KIRKMAN & SCOTT

WHAT DO YOU THINK OF MY FAMILY NEWSPAPER?
WELL...

I WAS JUST BROWSING THE FOOD AND TRAVEL SECTION, AND...
KIRKMAN & SCOTT

...IT SAYS MY SANDWICHES ARE DRY.
OUR FOOD CRITIC THINKS YOU SKIMP ON THE MAYO.
©2021, BABY BLUES BROS LLC DIST. BY KING FEATURES SYNDICATE 8-13

ARE YOU ENJOYING THE MacPHERSON TIMES FAMILY NEWSPAPER?
NO.

IN THE GOSSIP SECTION, IT SAYS THAT I CAN'T GO FIVE MINUTES WITHOUT TOOTING.

WHERE DID YOU HEAR THAT?
EVERYBODY HEARS IT.
©2021, BABY BLUES BROS LLC DIST. BY KING FEATURES SYNDICATE 8-14
KIRKMAN & SCOTT

GOT IT. THANKS, DAD.

HAMMIE, YOU'RE UP NEXT, SO LET'S GO OVER THE SIGNALS.
IF I DO THIS, IT MEANS "BUNT"...
IF I DO THIS, IT MEANS "STEAL"...
THIS IS "TAKE"...
..."HIT AND RUN..."
...AND "SWING AWAY."...
GOT IT. THANKS, DAD.
I THINK DAD IS TEACHING HAMMIE HOW TO UNDO A WEDGIE.
HE'S SUCH A THOUGHTFUL COACH.
KIRKMAN & SCOTT
8-1

I THINK IT'S TIME TO MOVE WREN INTO A REGULAR BED.
REALLY? WHY?
FLIP! FLIP! THUMP!
A LOWER DEGREE OF DIFFICULTY ON HER DISMOUNTS.
KIRKMAN & SCOTT
©2021, BABY BLUES BROS LLC DIST. BY KING FEATURES SYNDICATE 8-16

DARRYL, THE WASHER IS MAKING A FUNNY NOISE.
IS IT A "THUMP"? A "SQUEAL"? A "RATTLE"?
KIRKMAN & SCOTT
©2021, BABY BLUES BROS LLC DIST. BY KING FEATURES SYNDICATE 8-17

IT'S MORE LIKE A CRY FOR HELP.
UNDERSTANDABLE.

OOOOO-OOOO-OOO-OOO
SEE? THAT'S THE NOISE I WAS TELLING YOU ABOUT.
HMM...

HEY, SEARCHI, WHAT DOES IT MEAN WHEN YOUR WASHER STARTS MAKING STRANGE NOISES?
IT USUALLY MEANS THAT THE WARRANTY JUST RAN OUT.
KIRKMAN & SCOTT
©2021, BABY BLUES BROS LLC DIST. BY KING FEATURES SYNDICATE 8-18

WELL, SHOULD WE GO SHOPPING FOR A NEW WASHER AND DRYER?
GUESS SO.
KIRKMAN & SCOTT

WHEN?
PRETTY SOON.
LAUNDRY TENDS TO PILE UP FAST.
I SEE WHAT YOU MEAN.
©2021, BABY BLUES BROS LLC DIST. BY KING FEATURES SYNDICATE 8-19

I HATE TO ADMIT IT, BUT GETTING A NEW WASHER AND DRYER IS KIND OF EXCITING!

LOOK AT THIS ONE! TOUCH PANEL, SOIL-LEVEL SENSING, TWELVE SPECIALTY CYCLES, AND BLUETOOTH!
KIRKMAN & SCOTT
©2021, BABY BLUES BROS LLC DIST. BY KING FEATURES SYNDICATE 8-20

I HATE IT WHEN OUR APPLIANCES HAVE MORE COOL FEATURES THAN OUR CAR.
OOOH!

KIRKMAN & SCOTT
©2021, BABY BLUES BROS LLC DIST. BY KING FEATURES SYNDICATE 8-21

REALLY? YOU'RE PUTTING THIS ON SOCIAL MEDIA?
MAYTAG IS THE NEW FERRARI.

DWEEDLE! DWEEDLE! DWEEDLE!

OOPS!

SPOIT!

HELLO?

AACK!

WANDA?

OH, FOR PETE'S SAKE!

HELLO?

GOTCHA!

SORRY, DARRYL. I'M HAVING TROUBLE WITH MY PHONE.

BAD SIGNAL?

SUNBLOCK FINGERS.

SPF 9000



8-8

KIRKMAN & SCOTT

WHEN I WAS YOUR AGE, I WANTED TO BE A WRITER.
ARE YOU MAD THAT IT DIDN'T HAPPEN?

NO, BECAUSE I ENDED UP WITH THE BEST JOB IN THE WORLD!
©2021, BABY BLUES BROS LLC DIST. BY KING FEATURES SYNDICATE 8-23

LAUNDRY TECHNICIAN?
BEING A MOM!
KIRKMAN & SCOTT

I CAN'T FIND THE REMOTE, AND YOU HAD IT LAST.
HOW DO YOU KNOW?

BECAUSE YOU WERE SITTING IN THAT CHAIR, WEARING GREEN SHORTS AND EATING GRAPES WHILE WATCHING THE COMPANY PICNIC EPISODE OF "THE OFFICE" FOR THE ELEVENTH TIME.

©2021, BABY BLUES BROS LLC DIST. BY KING FEATURES SYNDICATE 8-24
BUT YOU CAN'T REMEMBER TO PICK UP YOUR SOCKS.
MAYBE I COULD IF THE REMOTE WAS IN THEM!
KIRKMAN & SCOTT

AREN'T YOU GOING TO HELP ME LOOK FOR THE REMOTE?
IT DEPENDS.

WHAT ARE YOU GOING TO WATCH?
UM... A DOCUMENTARY...
©2021, BABY BLUES BROS LLC DIST. BY KING FEATURES SYNDICATE 8-25

...THAT LOOKS A LOT LIKE A BASEBALL GAME.
YOU'RE ON YOUR OWN.
KIRKMAN & SCOTT

WHAT ARE YOU GUYS DOING IN HERE??
READING.

THE TV REMOTE IS STILL MISSING, AND YOU'RE **READING???**
KIRKMAN & SCOTT
©2021, BABY BLUES BROS LLC DIST. BY KING FEATURES SYNDICATE 8-26

OUR KIDS' PRIORITIES ARE OUT OF WHACK.
PROBABLY DUE TO BAD PARENTING.

HOOOOO!
WUAH!
WUAH!
WUAH!
YEEAH!

HAII-YAH!

YA!
YA!
YA!
YA!
YA!
YA!
YA!
YA!
YA!
8-22

HOO! HAW! YAH! YAH!
FFT! FFT!
FFT! FFT!

YEEAH!
HOOOO! WUAH! WUAH! WUAH!

KIRKMAN & SCOTT

THE WOMEN IN THIS FAMILY ARE ANNOYING.

WHO PUT THE REMOTE IN THE FRIDGE?
NO CONFESSION, EH? OKAY, THEN I'LL JUST LAUNCH MY OWN INVESTIGATION!
IF YOU DUST IT FOR FINGERPRINTS, THE PEANUT BUTTER ONES AREN'T MINE!
KIRKMAN & SCOTT
©2021, BABY BLUES BROS LLC DIST. BY KING FEATURES SYNDICATE 8-27

GUYS, I NEED YOU TO SORT THROUGH YOUR CLOSETS.
SEPARATE THE CLOTHES THAT STILL FIT FROM THE ONES THAT DON'T.
OKAY.
WHAT ABOUT ME?
YOU SEPARATE THE ONES THAT REEK FROM THE ONES THAT JUST STINK.
THIS COULD BE TRICKY...
KIRKMAN & SCOTT
©2021, BABY BLUES BROS LLC DIST. BY KING FEATURES SYNDICATE 8-28

MOM, I DROPPED YOUR PHONE IN THE TOILET AGAIN.
THAT'S FINE.

MOM, I USED UP ALL OF YOUR EXPENSIVE MAKEUP.
GOOD FOR YOU!
©2021, BABY BLUES BROS LLC DIST. BY KING FEATURES SYNDICATE 8-30
KIRKMAN & SCOTT
YOU ARE A COMPLETELY DIFFERENT PERSON WHEN SCHOOL STARTS BACK UP.
THE HOUSE SHALL BE RECLAIMED!
SMOOCH!

WE'RE HAVING STUDENT GOVERNMENT ELECTIONS THIS WEEK!
OH?
MILK

YES. AND I'M RUNNING FOR CLASS PRESIDENT!
HOW??
KIRKMAN & SCOTT
©2021, BABY BLUES BROS LLC DIST. BY KING FEATURES SYNDICATE 8-31
YOU DON'T **HAVE** ANY CLASS!
SAID THE CRITIC WITH FROOT LOOPS DRIBBLING OUT OF HIS MOUTH.

ZOE, I THINK YOU'D MAKE A WONDERFUL CLASS PRESIDENT.
REALLY?

YES! YOU'RE SMART AND COMPASSIONATE...
KIRKMAN & SCOTT

©2021, BABY BLUES BROS LLC DIST. BY KING FEATURES SYNDICATE 9-1
...WITH JUST A HINT OF DICTATOR.
FINISH UP. THE CARPOOL LEAVES IN FIVE.

ZOE IS GOING TO RUN FOR CLASS PRESIDENT.

WOW. A POLITICIAN IN THE FAMILY.

©2021, BABY BLUES BROS LLC DIST. BY KING FEATURES SYNDICATE 9-2
KIRKMAN & SCOTT
I HOPE THE PRESS DOESN'T DIG INTO YOUR PAST.
YOU'RE THE ONE WHO HAD A MULLET.

MOM, I'M GOING TO NEED SOME CAMPAIGN SUPPLIES.
OH, GOOD! YOU MADE A LIST.

MM-HMM... POSTER BOARD... MARKERS...
©2021, BABY BLUES BROS LLC DIST. BY KING FEATURES SYNDICATE 9-3
KIRKMAN & SCOTT
WE'RE NOT BUYING EVERYONE IN YOUR CLASS NEW iPHONES!
YOU'RE NEW TO POLITICS, AREN'T YOU?

ARE YOU WRITING YOUR CAMPAIGN SPEECH?
YOU BET.

WHAT'S YOUR PLATFORM?
MY WHAT?
©2021, BABY BLUES BROS LLC DIST. BY KING FEATURES SYNDICATE 9-4
KIRKMAN & SCOTT
WHAT ISSUES ARE YOU MOST CONCERNED ABOUT?
WELL, WINNING IS NUMBER ONE.

HEY, ZANE, WANT A COOKIE?
SURE.
OH, AND DO I HAVE YOUR VOTE FOR CLASS PRESIDENT?
MGMGLFG!
ALL ANSWERS, INCLUDING "MGMGLFP," COUNT AS A "YES."
©2021, BABY BLUES BROS LLC DIST. BY KING FEATURES SYNDICATE 9-6
KIRKMAN & SCOTT

STEPHIE, WHAT'S IT GOING TO TAKE FOR ME TO GET YOUR VOTE FOR CLASS PRESIDENT?
WILL YOU CUT THE CRUSTS OFF MY SANDWICH EVERY DAY? MY MOM WON'T DO IT.
KIRKMAN & SCOTT
©2021, BABY BLUES BROS LLC DIST. BY KING FEATURES SYNDICATE 9-7
LET ME CIRCLE BACK TO YOU ON THAT ONE.
TAKE THAT, YOU STUPID CRUST!

IF YOU GET THE COOL-GIRL VOTE, YOU'LL WIN FOR SURE.
I CAN'T TALK TO THEM!

THEY'RE COUNTRY-CLUB KIDS! THEIR PARENTS ARE RICH!
YOU GOTTA TRY.
©2021, BABY BLUES BROS LLC DIST. BY KING FEATURES SYNDICATE 9-8

WHO ELSE THINKS WE SHOULD HAVE POLO AT RECESS?
KIRKMAN & SCOTT

HOW'S LIFE ON THE CAMPAIGN TRAIL, ZOE?
EXHAUSTING.

YEP. THAT'S POLITICS—SHAKING HANDS AND KISSING BABIES.
©2021, BABY BLUES BROS LLC DIST. BY KING FEATURES SYNDICATE 9-9

I'VE NEVER SEEN THE PRESIDENT DO THAT.
DAD DOESN'T LIE.
KISS! KISS! KISS!
SHAKE! SHAKE! SHAKE!
KIRKMAN & SCOTT

IF I AM ELECTED, I WILL WORK HARD FOR YOU!
THERE WILL BE TATER TOTS ON EVERY LUNCH TRAY, WATER FOUNTAINS WITH DECENT PRESSURE...
...AND GUM-FREE DESK BOTTOMS!
YAY!
I LIKE HER VISION.
©2021, BABY BLUES BROS LLC DIST. BY KING FEATURES SYNDICATE 9-10
KIRKMAN & SCOTT

HOW'S THE CAMPAIGN FOR CLASS PRESIDENT GOING?
I DROPPED OUT OF THE RACE.
WHAT? WHY?
AS CLASS PRESIDENT, YOU SHOULD BE A PATIENT AND COOPERATIVE TYPE OF PERSON.
I'M MORE OF THE "SHUT-UP-AND-DO-IT-MY-WAY" TYPE OF PERSON.
I SECOND THAT!
KIRKMAN & SCOTT
©2021, BABY BLUES BROS LLC DIST. BY KING FEATURES SYNDICATE 9-11

AND THE WINNER OF THE ELECTION FOR CLASS PRESIDENT IS, OF COURSE...

...ZOE MacPHERSON!
YAY!!!
©2021, BABY BLUES BROS LLC DIST. BY KING FEATURES SYNDICATE 9-13

PLEASE! PLEASE! NO MORE APPLAUSE!
NO PROBLEM THERE.
KIRKMAN & SCOTT

SO, TODAY WE GET THE ELECTION RESULTS. I'M SOOO NERVOUS!
I THOUGHT YOU DROPPED OUT OF THE RACE.

I DID, BUT THEN I DROPPED BACK IN.
©2021, BABY BLUES BROS LLC DIST. BY KING FEATURES SYNDICATE 9-14
KIRKMAN & SCOTT

IT SEEMED LIKE A SHAME TO WASTE ALL THOSE THREATS AND BRIBES.
WE NEED TO TALK ABOUT PUBLIC SERVICE...

SNIFF!
SNIFF!
PEANUT BUTTER WITH NOTES OF EARTHWORM.
SNIFFFFF!
TREE SAP, DOG HAIR WITH A HINT OF ROQUEFORT.
ARMPIT-FORWARD,
SNIFF!
WITH MILD UNDERTONES OF BIKE GREASE AND SANDBOX.

THIS ISN'T LAUNDRY... IT'S A STINK JOURNAL.
TAKE MY ADVICE, AND SKIP THE LAST CHAPTER.
9-12
KIRKMAN & SCOTT
©2021, BABY BLUES BROS LLC DIST. BY KING FEATURES SYNDICATE

...AND OUR NEW CLASS PRESIDENT IS... JESSICA!
CLAP CLAP
CLAP CLAP

CONGRATULATIONS, JESSICA.
THANKS.
©2021, BABY BLUES BROS LLC DIST. BY KING FEATURES SYNDICATE 9-15
KIRKMAN & SCOTT
I COULDN'T BE HAPPIER FOR YOU.
YOU'RE SO SWEET!

I DIDN'T WIN THE ELECTION.
OH, I'M SORRY, SWEETIE.
THAT'S OKAY. THE IMPORTANT THING IS THAT I RAN A CLEAN RACE.
©2021, BABY BLUES BROS LLC DIST. BY KING FEATURES SYNDICATE 9-16
KIRKMAN & SCOTT
AND THAT I HAVE SOMEONE TO TAKE IT OUT ON LATER.
MOM, CAN I SLEEP OVER AT TRENT'S HOUSE FOR THE NEXT MONTH OR TWO?

YOUR SHIRT DOESN'T MATCH YOUR PANTS.

AND YOUR FACE DOESN'T MATCH YOUR HEAD, YOUR MOUTH DOESN'T MATCH YOUR TEETH, YOUR EYES...
ZOE...
©2021, BABY BLUES BROS LLC DIST. BY KING FEATURES SYNDICATE 9-17

...LEAVE YOUR BROTHER ALONE.
IT'S OKAY. I HAVE A THICK SISTER-CALLUS.
KIRKMAN & SCOTT

EEEEEK!
WHAT'S WRONG?

ONE OF HAMMIE'S DIRTY SOCKS HISSED AT ME AND RAN OFF!
THAT'S SILLY.
©2021, BABY BLUES BROS LLC DIST. BY KING FEATURES SYNDICATE 9-18

KIRKMAN & SCOTT
AT BEST, IT WOULD'VE HOPPED.
THAT'S NOT THE POINT!

DARRYL?
I! AM!
IN! THE!
GARAGE!!!!!

DARRYL?
I'M IN THE GARAGE.
DARRYL?
I'M IN THE GARAGE.
DARRYL?
I'M IN THE GARAGE!!
DARRYL?
I! AM!
IN! THE!
GARAGE!!!!!
9-19
©2021, BABY BLUES BROS LLC DIST. BY KING FEATURES SYNDICATE
HI. WHATCHA' DOIN'?
I JUST MET A DOG NAMED DARRYL.
KIRKMAN & SCOTT

I DON'T KNOW WHAT I WANT TO BE WHEN I GROW UP.

YOU'LL PROBABLY BE A HARDWORKING TAXPAYER WITH A STEADY JOB AND A FAMILY OF YOUR OWN, LIKE ME.
©2021, BABY BLUES BROS LLC DIST. BY KING FEATURES SYNDICATE 9-20
IS THERE AN OPTION B?

MOM, I'M NOT SURE WHAT I WANT TO BE WHEN I GROW UP.

ALL YOU NEED TO DO IS FOLLOW YOUR HEART.
©2021, BABY BLUES BROS LLC DIST. BY KING FEATURES SYNDICATE 9-21

WHAT IF MY HEART'S AN IDIOT?
:SIGH: IT WOULDN'T BE THE FIRST.

ZOE, WHAT ARE GOING TO BE WHEN YOU GROW UP?
A DOCTOR OR A TEACHER.
I WANT TO MAKE A POSITIVE IMPACT ON THE WORLD.
HOW COULD I MAKE A POSITIVE IMPACT?
LEAVING ME ALONE WOULD BE A GOOD START.
©2021, BABY BLUES BROS LLC DIST. BY KING FEATURES SYNDICATE 9-22
KIRKMAN & SCOTT

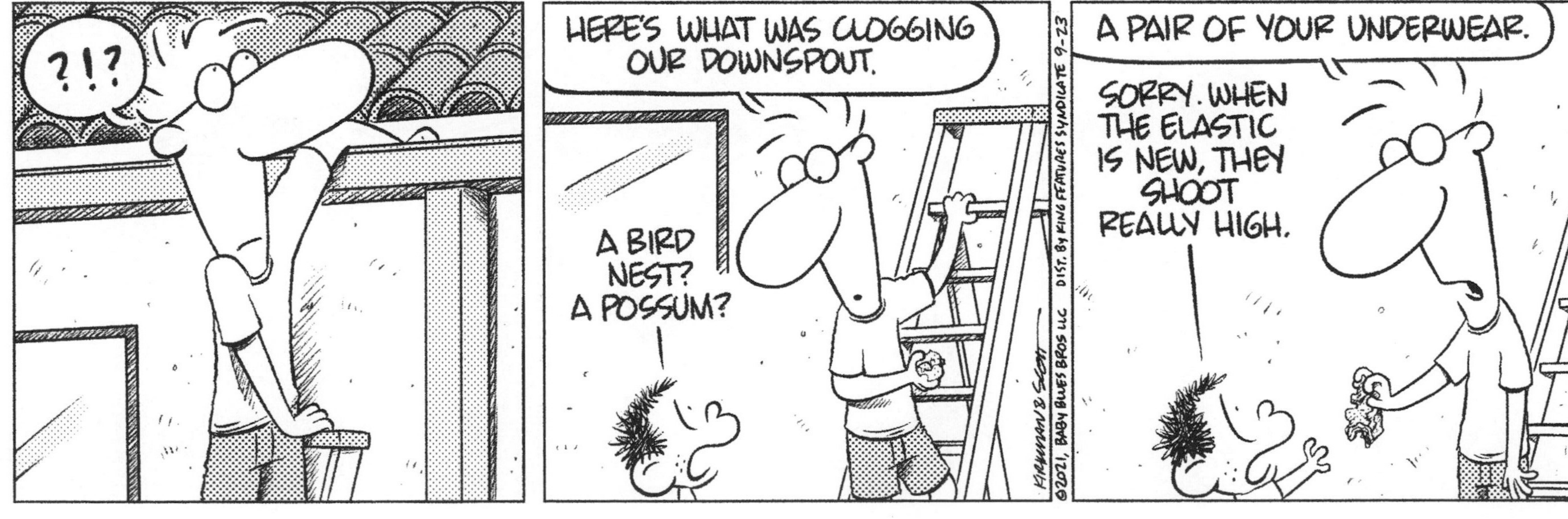
?!?
HERE'S WHAT WAS CLOGGING OUR DOWNSPOUT.
A BIRD NEST? A POSSUM?
A PAIR OF YOUR UNDERWEAR.
SORRY. WHEN THE ELASTIC IS NEW, THEY SHOOT REALLY HIGH.
©2021, BABY BLUES BROS LLC DIST. BY KING FEATURES SYNDICATE 9-23
KIRKMAN & SCOTT

YOU FAILED A MATH QUIZ??
MOM, IT'S NOT MY FAULT!

THERE WERE TEN CORRECT ANSWERS, AND **BILLIONS** OF WRONG ONES.
KIRKMAN & SCOTT

©2021, BABY BLUES BROS LLC DIST. BY KING FEATURES SYNDICATE 9-24
WHAT DOES THAT H–
I WAS CLEARLY OUTNUMBERED.

DID YOU FINISH YOUR BOOK REPORT?
YEP.

DID YOU ACTUALLY **READ** THE BOOK THIS TIME?
MORE OR LESS.
©2021, BABY BLUES BROS LLC DIST. BY KING FEATURES SYNDICATE 9-25
HOW MUCH LESS?
I TALK A LOT ABOUT THE COVER.
KIRKMAN & SCOTT

LET'S GO, GUYS.

TIME FOR BATHS.

AW!

HANG ON, HAMMIE.

SHAKE
SHAKE
SHAKE

SHAKE
SHAKE
SHAKE

SHAKE
SHAKE
SHAKE

9-26

THAT'S BETTER.

I'LL TELL MOM THAT I DON'T NEED A BATH AFTER ALL!



KIRKMAN & SCOTT

HIKE!
TWEET!
TWEET!
TWEET!
©2021, BABY BLUES BROS LLC DIST. BY KING FEATURES SYNDICATE 9-27

GO LONG, HAMMIE!
TWEET!
TWEET!
TWEET!

TWEEET!
ANYBODY ELSE GETTING A HEADACHE?
WE NEED A NEW REF.
KIRKMAN & SCOTT

TWEET!
TWEET!
TWEET!

PENALTY ON HAMMIE!
FOR WHAT??
©2021, BABY BLUES BROS LLC DIST. BY KING FEATURES SYNDICATE 9-28

STEPPING ON MY TOE!
THAT WAS LAST WEEK!
TOUGH REFEREE.
KIRKMAN & SCOTT

GO, WREN! GO!
TOUCHDOWN!
YAY!

LOOK! SHE SPIKED THE BALL!
I TAUGHT HER THAT.
©2021, BABY BLUES BROS LLC DIST. BY KING FEATURES SYNDICATE 9-29
AND NOW SHE'S MOONING US.
I COULDN'T BE PROUDER.
KIRKMAN & SCOTT

I'M TRYING SOMETHING DIFFERENT TODAY.
WHAT IS IT?
ZOE AND HAMMIE ARE MAKING THEIR OWN LUNCHES.
THAT'S A GREAT-
KIRKMAN & SCOTT
©2021, BABY BLUES BROS LLC DIST. BY KING FEATURES SYNDICATE 9-30
...IDEA.
I'LL GET THE POWER WASHER.

BEDTIME. PICK UP THESE TOYS.
WILL DO!

KIRKMAN & SCOTT
©2021, BABY BLUES BROS LLC DIST. BY KING FEATURES SYNDICATE 10-1

AND **NOT** WITH THE JEDI MIND TRICK.
YOU NEVER GIVE IT ENOUGH TIME.

HOW MANY TIMES HAVE I TOLD YOU TWO TO STOP BICKERING?

AROUND ELEVEN JILLION.

REALLY? THAT SEEMS LOW TO ME.
I THINK IT'S ABOUT AVERAGE, UNLESS...
©2021, BABY BLUES BROS LLC DIST. BY KING FEATURES SYNDICATE 10-2

...ARE YOU TALKING LIFETIME OR JUST TODAY?
JUST TODAY.
OH, OKAY. THEN HE'S RIGHT.
KIRKMAN & SCOTT

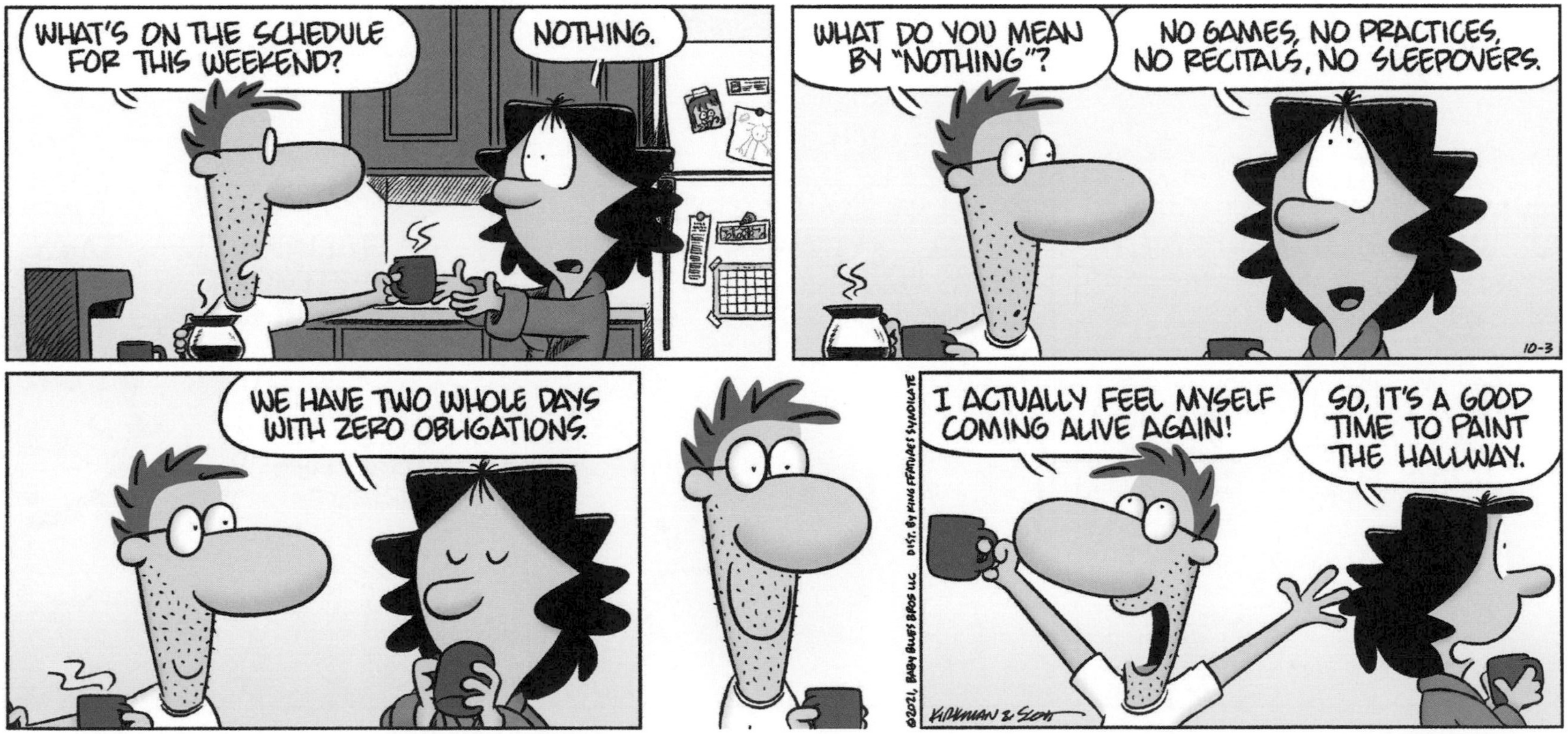

WHAT'S ON THE SCHEDULE FOR THIS WEEKEND?

NOTHING.

WHAT DO YOU MEAN BY "NOTHING"?

NO GAMES, NO PRACTICES, NO RECITALS, NO SLEEPOVERS.

10-3

WE HAVE TWO WHOLE DAYS WITH ZERO OBLIGATIONS.

I ACTUALLY FEEL MYSELF COMING ALIVE AGAIN!

SO, IT'S A GOOD TIME TO PAINT THE HALLWAY.



KIRKMAN & SCOTT

MOM! I'M STUDENT OF THE WEEK!
WOW! THAT'S GREAT!

THIS IS DEFINITELY GOING ON THE FRIDGE.
©2021, BABY BLUES BROS LLC DIST. BY KING FEATURES SYNDICATE 10-4

I'LL PUT IT RIGHT NEXT TO HAMMIE'S THIRD AND FINAL WARNING FROM THE PRINCIPAL.
MINE HAS MORE EXCLAMATION POINTS.
KIRKMAN & SCOTT

TODAY, A BUNCH OF KIDS CALLED ME "TEACHER'S PET" BECAUSE I'M STUDENT OF THE WEEK.
OH DEAR.

I'M SO, SO, SO SORRY, ZOE!
?
KIRKMAN & SCOTT
©2021, BABY BLUES BROS LLC DIST. BY KING FEATURES SYNDICATE 10-5

YOU SHOULDN'T LET IT GET YOU DOWN.
IT DIDN'T... UNTIL NOW.

SOME KIDS CALLED ZOE "TEACHER'S PET" AT SCHOOL TODAY.
OUCH.

I NEVER HAD TO DEAL WITH THAT, BECAUSE I WAS THE "BAD BOY" AT HER AGE.
KIRKMAN & SCOTT

DID YOU RUN WITH SCISSORS?
NO, BUT I WALKED VERY BRISKLY WITH THEM.
©2021, BABY BLUES BROS LLC DIST. BY KING FEATURES SYNDICATE 10-6

NOW THE KIDS ARE CALLING ME "GOODY TWO-SHOES."
OH, SWEETIE...

THEY'RE JUST JEALOUS BECAUSE YOU'RE A GOOD STUDENT.
IT STILL HURTS.
KIRKMAN & SCOTT

I MAY NEED YOU TO ROUGH UP SOME FOURTH-GRADERS.
I'LL NEED TIME TO TRAIN.
©2021, BABY BLUES BROS LLC DIST. BY KING FEATURES SYNDICATE 10-7

HAMMIE, I NEED YOUR HELP.
WITH WHAT?

I'M SICK OF BEING CALLED "GOODY TWO-SHOES" AT SCHOOL.
I SEE.
©2021, BABY BLUES BROS LLC DIST. BY KING FEATURES SYNDICATE 10-8
TEACH ME YOUR WAYS.
I'VE BEEN WAITING FOR THIS MOMENT MY WHOLE LIFE!

OKAY, LESSON ONE ON BEING BAD.
I'M WAY AHEAD OF YOU.

HOW? YOU LOOK LIKE THE SAME "RULE FOLLOWER" TO ME.
©2021, BABY BLUES BROS LLC DIST. BY KING FEATURES SYNDICATE 10-9
I'M WEARING A SUMMER-WEIGHT SWEATER IN OCTOBER!
BABY STEPS... BABY STEPS...

BEHOLD! MY NEWEST GRAPHIC NOVEL!
DON'T TELL ME... ANOTHER ROBOT SISTER COMIC?
Robot Sister
YES! HOW DID YOU KNOW?
IT'S THE ONLY CHARACTER YOU EVER WRITE ABOUT?
SO, IN THIS EPISODE, ROBOT SISTER HAS STOLEN THE GOLDEN FUDGESICLE!
THAT DOESN'T MAKE ANY SENSE.
THE HANDSOME SCIENTIST (ME) MUST HATCH A BRILLIANT PLAN TO GET THE GOLDEN FUDGESICLE BEFORE IT'S TIME FOR DESSERT!
SO WHAT'S THIS BRILLIANT PLAN?
Look over there!
Huh?
YOINK!
Goldn Fudjsikl
THAT'S YOUR IDEA OF A BRILLIANT PLAN?
HE'S JUST OUTSMARTING ROBOT SISTER, NOT THE JOKER.

10-24



KIRKMAN & SCOTT

ZOE, WHY AREN'T YOU EATING?
ONLY A GOODY-TWO-SHOES EATS VEGETABLES.

OH, SO YOU'RE LOOKING FOR SOME STREET CRED?
YEAH. HAMMIE IS MENTORING ME.
©2021, BABY BLUES BROS LLC DIST. BY KING FEATURES SYNDICATE 10-11

SCARIER WORDS HAVE NEVER BEEN SPOKEN.
NOW GO UN-TIDY YOUR ROOM.
KIRKMAN & SCOTT

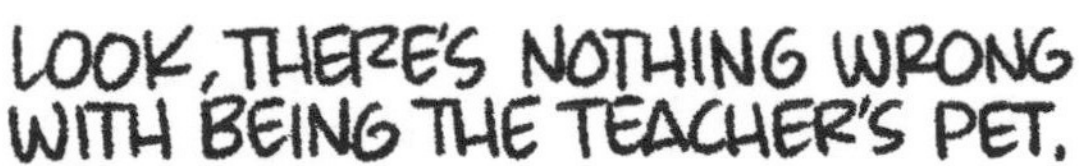
LOOK, THERE'S NOTHING WRONG WITH BEING THE TEACHER'S PET.

WHO CARES IF THEY CALL YOU "GOODY-TWO-SHOES"? JUST BE ZOE. BE YOU.
©2021, BABY BLUES BROS LLC DIST. BY KING FEATURES SYNDICATE 10-12

CAN I STILL BE A PAIN IN THE BUTT AT HOME?
I'D EXPECT NOTHING LESS.
KIRKMAN & SCOTT

KIRKMAN & SCOTT

MY BEDROOM COLORS DON'T UPLIFT ME.
I DIDN'T KNOW THAT WAS A THING.
©2021, BABY BLUES BROS LLC DIST. BY KING FEATURES SYNDICATE 10-13

ZOE AND I ARE GOING TO PAINT HER ROOM.

SO WE'RE OFF TO BUY PAINT, ROLLERS, TARPS AND CHERRY SODA.

CHERRY SODA IS A PAINTING SUPPLY?
MORE OF A TRADITION.
AND THE ONLY REASON I GO WITH HIM TO THE HARDWARE STORE.
©2021, BABY BLUES BROS LLC DIST. BY KING FEATURES SYNDICATE 10-14
KIRKMAN & SCOTT

OKAY, ZOE. PICK A COLOR.
WHOA.

THERE ARE SO MANY CHOICES! THIS COULD TAKE HOURS!
YEAH.
KIRKMAN & SCOTT
©2021, BABY BLUES BROS LLC DIST. BY KING FEATURES SYNDICATE 10-15

I'M GOING TO NEED A PATIO CHAIR FOR THIS.

WELL? WHAT DO YOU THINK?
I LOVE IT.

THIS NEW COLOR TOTALLY INSPIRES ME!
KIRKMAN & SCOTT
©2021, BABY BLUES BROS LLC DIST. BY KING FEATURES SYNDICATE 10-16

GOOD. NOW HELP ME CLEAN UP.
UH-OH. INSPIRATION IS FADING...

KNOCK OFF THE ATTITUDE, UNDERSTAND?

HAMMIE! GET OUT OF MY ROOM!
DON'T TOUCH MY STUFF, WREN!
YOU GUYS BETTER LEAVE ME ALONE, OR ELSE!
ZOE, CAN I SPEAK TO YOU FOR A SECOND?
KNOCK OFF THE ATTITUDE, UNDERSTAND?
10-17
©2021, BABY BLUES BROS LLC DIST. BY KING FEATURES SYNDICATE
MOM YELLED AT ME!
KIRKMAN & SCOTT

WHAT ARE YOU DOING, MOM?
CLEANING.

THERE ARE LOTS AND LOTS OF DUST BUNNIES UNDER HERE.
©2021, BABY BLUES BROS LLC DIST. BY KING FEATURES SYNDICATE 10-18

WE'RE INFESTED.
WITH SOMETHING WORSE THAN YOU?

MOM SAID THAT WE HAVE DUST BUNNIES.
SO...?

SO, WHO KNOWS WHAT OTHER HIDEOUS DUST CREATURES WE HAVE AROUND HERE.
©2021, BABY BLUES BROS LLC DIST. BY KING FEATURES SYNDICATE 10-19

ALTHOUGH, DUST SKUNKS WOULD BE KIND OF FUN.
YOU'RE THE DUST SKUNK.

HEADS UP, WREN. WE HAVE DUST BUNNIES.
THEY'RE PROBABLY NOT THE RADIOACTIVE-VAMPIRE KIND, BUT YOU NEVER KNOW.

FOR SOME REASON, SHE'S NOT GOING TO SLEEP.

SHHH...
I'M HUNTING DUST BUNNIES.
HAMMIE...

...DUST BUNNIES ARE JUST CLUMPS OF DUST AND HAIR. THEY'RE NOT DANGEROUS.

BESIDES, YOU LOVE FILTH!
ONLY WHEN I'M THE CAUSE OF IT.

MOM! WE HAVE A BOOK FAIR NEXT WEEK!
FUN!

I USED TO LOVE BOOK FAIRS WHEN I WAS YOUR AGE.
©2021, BABY BLUES BROS LLC DIST. BY KING FEATURES SYNDICATE 10-22

THEY HAD BOOKS BACK THEN??
I DON'T KNOW WHETHER TO BELIEVE HER OR NOT.

TODAY, TRENT TOLD ME TO PULL HIS FINGER.

SO I DID, AND GUESS WHAT HAPPENED.
©2021, BABY BLUES BROS LLC DIST. BY KING FEATURES SYNDICATE 10-23

DAD IS PSYCHIC.

MOM?

MOM?
10-10

MOM?
MOM?
MOM?

MOM?

MOM?

DO ANYTHING INTERESTING TODAY?
I YELLED "IN HERE" FROM NINE DIFFERENT ROOMS.

DAD, CAN WE CARVE OUR PUMPKINS TONIGHT?
SURE.
PLEASE?
GO PUT ON SOME CLOTHES YOU CAN GET DIRTY.
©2021, BABY BLUES BROS LLC DIST. BY KING FEATURES SYNDICATE 10-25
KIRKMAN & SCOTT
YOU MUST BE PRETTY CONFUSED RIGHT NOW.
WHAT KIND OF CLOTHES CAN'T GET DIRTY??
NOW, LIGHTLY DRAW THE FACE YOU WANT TO CARVE ON YOUR PUMPKIN.
I'M GONNA DO A SCARY ONE!
I'M GOING TO DRAW SOMETHING GOOFY!
©2021, BABY BLUES BROS LLC DIST. BY KING FEATURES SYNDICATE 10-26
KIRKMAN & SCOTT
TURN THIS WAY, AND MAKE YOUR NORMAL FACE.

MY PUMPKIN WILL BE SO GREAT!

IT'S GONNA HAVE A SKULL WITH A GIANT SNAKE CRAWLING OUT OF THE EYEHOLE!
KIRKMAN & SCOTT
©2021, BABY BLUES BROS LLC DIST. BY KING FEATURES SYNDICATE 10-27

IT LOOKS LIKE A CAT.
CATS ARE THE ONLY THING I KNOW HOW TO DRAW.

WHAT'S YOUR HALLOWEEN COSTUME GOING TO BE THIS YEAR?
NOT SURE.

I'LL PROBABLY JUST DO WHAT I DID LAST YEAR.
©2021, BABY BLUES BROS LLC DIST. BY KING FEATURES SYNDICATE 10-28

WAIT UNTIL THE BIG DAY, THEN BEG MOM TO WHIP UP SOME-THING AWESOME AT THE LAST MINUTE?
YEAH.
NO!!
KIRKMAN & SCOTT

MOM, FOR DINNER TONIGHT I'LL HAVE A BAG OF FUN-SIZE SNICKERS.
IS THAT SO?

YEAH. I HAVE TO GET THE OL' TUMMY IN SHAPE FOR THE CANDY AVALANCHE ON SUNDAY.
KIRKMAN & SCOTT

OH, AND FOR DESSERT, I'LL HAVE A FEW HANDFULS OF M&M'S.
I'LL GET RIGHT ON THAT.
©2021, BABY BLUES BROS LLC DIST. BY KING FEATURES SYNDICATE 10-29

WHEEEE! HERE GOES THE AIRPLANE!

WHEEE—
BLARGH!
KIRKMAN & SCOTT
SORRY ABOUT THE TARMAC.
GO RENT A CARPET CLEANER, FLYBOY.
©2021, BABY BLUES BROS LLC DIST. BY KING FEATURES SYNDICATE 10-30

WHERE ARE ALL OF THE CARVING TOOLS?

DONE!

KIRKMAN & SCOTT 10-31

QUIT TOUCHING ME!
OW!
I NEED SOME COFFEE.
JOE BUZZ JAVA COFFEE
DRIVE THRU
KIRKMAN & SCOTT
I'M SERIOUS! KNOCK IT OFF BEFORE I—
KEE-RUNCH!
©2021, BABY BLUES BROS LLC DIST. BY KING FEATURES SYNDICATE 11-1
DID WE JUST HIT JOE BUZZ?
I DON'T GET PAID ENOUGH FOR THIS JOB.
MOM KILLED JOE BUZZ!

MOM! DID YOU JUST CRASH INTO A JOE BUZZ?
NO.
BZZT CRACKLE
DID YOU ALMOST CRASH INTO A JOE BUZZ?
NO, I JUST BUMPED INTO A CONCRETE POLE.
©2021, BABY BLUES BROS LLC DIST. BY KING FEATURES SYNDICATE 11-2
BUT WITHOUT THE POLE, YOU WOULD HAVE CRASHED INTO A JOE BUZZ?
ENOUGH QUESTIONS!!
KIRKMAN & SCOTT

I'D LIKE A MEDIUM SOY LATTE, PLEASE.

BZT
DID YOU JUST HIT OUR POLE?
YES, BUT THERE WERE EXTENUATING CIRCUMSTANCES.
©2021, BABY BLUES BROS LLC DIST. BY KING FEATURES SYNDICATE 11-3
MOM JUST CALLED YOU "EXTENUATING."
JUST GET ME THE LATTE, PLEASE!
IS THAT A CUSS WORD?
KIRKMAN & SCOTT

LET ME TELL DAD ABOUT OUR LITTLE ACCIDENT.

YOU MEAN OUR TERRIFYING NEAR-DEATH EXPERIENCE?
KIRKMAN & SCOTT
©2021, BABY BLUES BROS LLC DIST. BY KING FEATURES SYNDICATE 11-4

WE JUST TAPPED A POLE AT HALF A MILE PER HOUR!
SEE WHY YOU HAVE ONLY SIX INSTAGRAM FOLLOWERS?

HI, GUYS! WHAT'S NEW?
HAMMIE!
MOM CRASHED THE CAR!

SHE BARRELED INTO A CONCRETE POLE AT FULL SPEED AND TOTALED THE CAR!
IT WAS AWFUL.
©2021, BABY BLUES BROS LLC DIST. BY KING FEATURES SYNDICATE 11-5

I BUMPED INTO A POLE!
PLUS, SHE LACKS DRAMA.
KIRKMAN & SCOTT

SO WHAT REALLY HAPPENED TO THE CAR?
I BUMPED INTO A POLE AT JOE BUZZ.

WAS THERE ANY DAMAGE?
NOT MUCH.
WAS ANYONE HURT?
NO.
©2021, BABY BLUES BROS LLC DIST. BY KING FEATURES SYNDICATE 11-6

WILL THE KIDS EVER LET YOU LIVE IT DOWN?
WE'RE THROUGH HERE!
KIRKMAN & SCOTT

LOOK OUT BELOW!!

KA-POW!

©2021, BABY BLUES BROS LLC DIST. BY KING FEATURES SYNDICATE

11-7

ANOTHER TOTAL ACCIDENT, I ASSUME?

I HAVE THE WORST LUCK.

SOB!

'SUP?
I HAVE TO WRITE A REPORT ON STUPID THANKSGIVING.

IT JUST GETS IN THE WAY OF THE REAL HOLIDAYS!
KIRKMAN & SCOTT
©2021, BABY BLUES BROS LLC DIST. BY KING FEATURES SYNDICATE 11-8

MY BROTHER, THE PILGRIM DENIER.
Thanksgiving is a speed bump between Halloween and Christmas.

ARE YOU STILL WORKING ON THAT REPORT?
OF COURSE.

WE HAVE TO INCLUDE A LIST OF THINGS THAT WE'RE THANKFUL FOR.
©2021, BABY BLUES BROS LLC DIST. BY KING FEATURES SYNDICATE 11-9

BOOGERS?? WHAT ABOUT SISTERS?
FURTHER DOWN THE LIST, NEAR BATHING.
KIRKMAN & SCOTT

...AND HERE YOU SHOULD SAY, "THE PILGRIMS ATE TURKEY BECAUSE IT WAS ON SALE."

AND BESIDES, IT WAS TOO HARD TO STUFF A MOOSE.
THAT MAKES SENSE.
©2021, BABY BLUES BROS LLC DIST. BY KING FEATURES SYNDICATE 11-10

THANKS FOR HELPING ME WITH MY REPORT.
YOUR GRADE WILL BE THANKS ENOUGH.
KIRKMAN & SCOTT

FIRST, IT WAS COVID WEIGHT, THEN DELTA COVID...

...AND NOW WE'RE HEADED INTO THE HOLIDAYS!
©2021, BABY BLUES BROS LLC DIST. BY KING FEATURES SYNDICATE 11-11

MY HIPS MIGHT AS WELL WAVE THE WHITE FLAG.
I WOULDN'T MIND SEEING THAT.
KIRKMAN & SCOTT

THERE! WHAT A CUTE OUTFIT, WREN!

NO! NAKEY!
KIRKMAN & SCOTT

PRESCHOOL PROMISES TO BE INTERESTING.
I MAY HAVE TO STAPLE HER INTO HER CLOTHES.
©2021, BABY BLUES BROS LLC DIST. BY KING FEATURES SYNDICATE 11-12

DELICIOUS APPLE CIDER FOR SALE!
MINE IS BETTER!
Fresh Cider ¢25

PLUS, I'LL GIVE YOU A FREE BUG WITH EVERY CUP!

THE COMPETITION IS FIERCE ON THIS STREET.
NOT FOR THE OTHER KID.
©2021, BABY BLUES BROS LLC DIST. BY KING FEATURES SYNDICATE 11-13
KIRKMAN & SCOTT

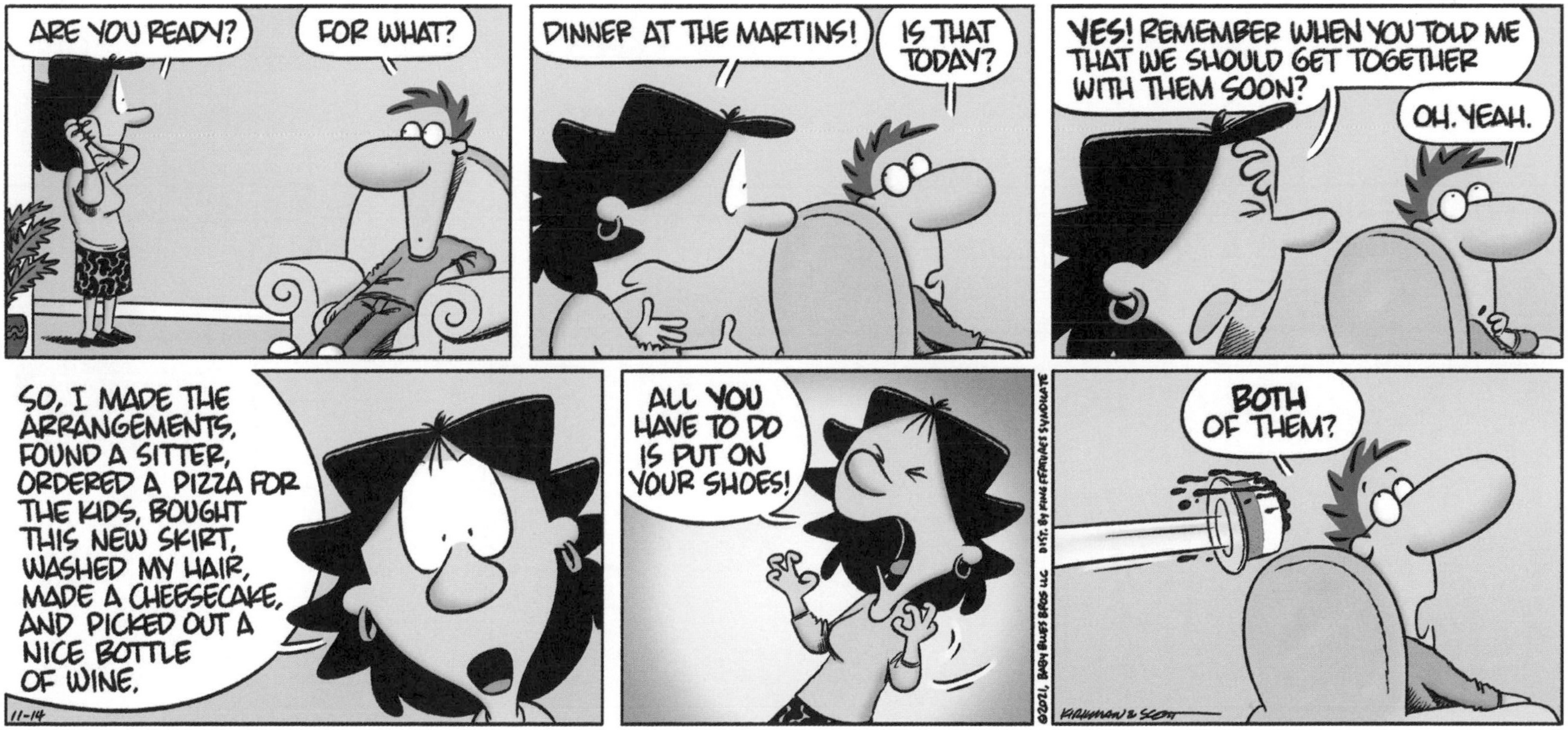

ARE YOU READY?

FOR WHAT?

DINNER AT THE MARTINS!

IS THAT TODAY?

YES! REMEMBER WHEN YOU TOLD ME THAT WE SHOULD GET TOGETHER WITH THEM SOON?

OH. YEAH.

SO, I MADE THE ARRANGEMENTS, FOUND A SITTER, ORDERED A PIZZA FOR THE KIDS, BOUGHT THIS NEW SKIRT, WASHED MY HAIR, MADE A CHEESECAKE, AND PICKED OUT A NICE BOTTLE OF WINE.

ALL YOU HAVE TO DO IS PUT ON YOUR SHOES!

BOTH OF THEM?

11-14



KIRKMAN & SCOTT

SO, THERE'S A JOB OPENING AT WORK THAT I MIGHT APPLY FOR.
I WOULD MAKE MORE MONEY, BUT IT WOULD MEAN MORE STRESS.
ARE WE TALKING VACATION-AT-DISNEY-WORLD MONEY, OR LET'S-REUPHOLSTER-THE-COUCH MONEY?
THE SECOND ONE
NOT WORTH IT!
KIRKMAN & SCOTT
©2021, BABY BLUES BROS LLC DIST. BY KING FEATURES SYNDICATE 11-15

IF I GOT THE NEW POSITION, I WOULD BE MANAGING A GROUP OF THIRTEEN PEOPLE.
DOES THAT SCARE YOU?
A LITTLE.
I CAN BARELY GET MY KIDS TO DO WHAT I ASK.
WHO CAN?
KIRKMAN & SCOTT
©2021, BABY BLUES BROS LLC DIST. BY KING FEATURES SYNDICATE 11-16

WELL, I'M INTERVIEWING FOR THE NEW POSITION TODAY!
BE SURE TO SIT UP STRAIGHT.

AND TRY NOT TO SAY "UM" BEFORE EVERY SENTENCE.
©2021, BABY BLUES BROS LLC DIST. BY KING FEATURES SYNDICATE 11-17

HAMMIE? ANY TIPS?
IF YOU TOOT, POINT AT SOMEBODY ELSE.
KIRKMAN & SCOTT

I GOT THE JOB!

YOU'RE LOOKING AT THE NEW SENIOR WESTERN REGIONAL ASSISTANT DIRECTOR OF LIMITED BUDGETARY INTEGRATION AND PLANNING.
©2021, BABY BLUES BROS LLC DIST. BY KING FEATURES SYNDICATE 11-18

DO YOU HAVE TO KNOW HOW TO SPELL ALL THAT?
HOW DO YOU THINK I GOT THE JOB?
KIRKMAN & SCOTT

JUST! LIE! DOWN! WREN!

IF YOU DON'T GET A NAP, YOU'LL BE TIRED AND CRANKY!
©2021, BABY BLUES BROS LLC DIST. BY KING FEATURES SYNDICATE 11-19
I SHOULD KNOW.
RUN! IT'S NO-NAP MOM!
KIRKMAN & SCOTT

GUYS! "A CHARLIE BROWN THANKSGIVING" IS ON!
HA! I LOVE IT WHEN SHE PULLS THE FOOTBALL AWAY AT THE LAST SECOND, AND HE
AAAUGH!
©2021, BABY BLUES BROS LLC DIST. BY KING FEATURES SYNDICATE 11-20
HOW ABOUT A SPOILER ALERT NEXT TIME?
RIGHT. SORRY.
KIRKMAN & SCOTT

...SYRUP...

BUTTER...

...SYRUP...
©2021, BABY BLUES BROS LLC DIST. BY KING FEATURES SYNDICATE 11-21

...AND SOME WHIPPED CREAM!
SQZZK!

YOUR PANCAKE SHOULD BE DOWN SHORTLY.

WHAT ARE YOU GUYS DOING?
TRYING TO FIND THE HIDDEN OBJECT.
I USED TO LOVE THOSE BOOKS.
©2021, BABY BLUES BROS LLC DIST. BY KING FEATURES SYNDICATE 11-22
KIRKMAN & SCOTT
-SIGH!- SOMETIMES I MISS MY CHILDHOOD.
I HEAR YA, SISTER.

BE CAREFUL. SANTA'S WATCHING.
HOW DO YOU KNOW?
BECAUSE THANKSGIVING WEEK IS WHEN HE STARTS OFFICIAL SURVEILLANCE OPERATIONS.
WAIT. I THOUGHT HE WAS WATCHING ALL THE TIME.
©2021, BABY BLUES BROS LLC DIST. BY KING FEATURES SYNDICATE 11-23
NOPE. ANY GOOD BEHAVIOR BETWEEN JANUARY AND MID-NOVEMBER DOESN'T COUNT.
WHY DON'T THEY TEACH US THIS STUFF IN SCHOOL??
KIRKMAN & SCOTT

...TWO... THREE... FOUR...

MY SISTER IS A DOPE!
SHE'S MY BIGGEST FOE!
IF I HAD A HAMMER,
I'D DROP IT ON HER TOE!
TWANG! BWANG!
KIRKMAN & SCOTT

I'M ASKING SANTA FOR AN AMPLIFIER THIS YEAR.
DON'T GET YOUR HOPES UP.
©2021, BABY BLUES BROS LLC DIST. BY KING FEATURES SYNDICATE 11-24

YOU'RE UP EARLY!
WELL, IT'S A BUSY HOLIDAY...

... A PACKED SCHEDULE.
RIGHT!
KIRKMAN & SCOTT
©2021, BABY BLUES BROS LLC DIST. BY KING FEATURES SYNDICATE 11-25

FIRST, WE'LL MAKE THE PIES...
I MEANT THE FOOTBALL SCHEDULE.

BZZZZZZZZZZZ

HAMMIE, CAN YOU PULL THE CLOTHES OUT OF THE DRYER AND PUT THEM ON THE COUCH?
OKAY!

MAKE SURE YOU GET THEM ALL!
WILL DO!
©2021, BABY BLUES BROS LLC DIST. BY KING FEATURES SYNDICATE

THERE'S A BASKET RIGHT NEXT TO THE DRYER!

A BASKET FOR WHAT?
KIRKMAN & SCOTT 11-28

WHO UNPLUGGED MY PHONE CHARGER??
IT WAS ME.

WHY WOULD YOU DO THAT??
SO YOU WOULD PAY ATTENTION TO ME INSTEAD OF YOUR PHONE.
©2021, BABY BLUES BROS LLC DIST. BY KING FEATURES SYNDICATE 11-26

IF THIS IS MY PUNISHMENT, IT'S WORKING.
KIRKMAN & SCOTT

TOUCHDOWN! WE WIN!!

LICK!
KIRKMAN & SCOTT
©2021, BABY BLUES BROS LLC DIST. BY KING FEATURES SYNDICATE 11-27

I'LL BE GLAD WHEN YOU GET THE HANG OF HIGH-FIVES.

©2021, BABY BLUES BROS LLC DIST. BY KING FEATURES SYNDICATE 11-29
DOES ANYBODY HAVE SOMETHING BESIDES A TURKEY SANDWICH TO TRADE??
KIRKMAN & SCOTT

THIS SUPPLY-CHAIN DISRUPTION REALLY HAS ME WORRIED.
CARGO SHIPS ARE BACKED UP AT EVERY PORT.

SANTA HAS HIS WORK CUT OUT FOR HIM THIS YEAR.
YOU GOT THAT RIGHT.
©2021, BABY BLUES BROS LLC DIST. BY KING FEATURES SYNDICATE 11-30

KIRKMAN & SCOTT

SIGH!
STILL NO DELIVERIES.

I'M WORRIED ABOUT STUFF ARRIVING ON TIME.
I'LL LOOK AT THE TRACKING APP.
©2021, BABY BLUES BROS LLC DIST. BY KING FEATURES SYNDICATE 12-1

WHAT DOES IT SAY?
KIRKMAN & SCOTT

WHAT ARE YOU GETTING MOM FOR CHRISTMAS?

THAT'S UP TO SANTA, NOT ME.
KIRKMAN & SCOTT
©2021, BABY BLUES BROS LLC DIST. BY KING FEATURES SYNDICATE 12-2

YOU HAVEN'T EVEN THOUGHT ABOUT IT, HAVE YOU?
DON'T YOU HAVE HOMEWORK?

I THINK WE SHOULD SEND OUT CHRISTMAS CARDS THIS YEAR.
KIRKMAN & SCOTT
©2021, BABY BLUES BROS LLC DIST. BY KING FEATURES SYNDICATE 12-3
YOU MEAN I SHOULD SEND OUT CHRISTMAS CARDS THIS YEAR.
WE COMMUNICATE SO WELL.

IF WE'RE DOING CHRISTMAS CARDS, WE NEED TO GET STARTED.
AGREED.
LET'S KEEP IT SIMPLE AND JUST DO ONE OF THOSE FAMILY PHOTO CARDS.
GOOD IDEA.
©2021, BABY BLUES BROS LLC DIST. BY KING FEATURES SYNDICATE 12-4
I'LL GET THE KIDS READY, AND YOU TIDY UP THE LIVING ROOM.
CAN I USE THE LEAF BLOWER?
KIRKMAN & SCOTT

GZZZZZZZZZKT!

KA-BOOM!

SHOOSHOOSHOOSHOO

YOU LOOK DISAPPOINTED.

I WAS EXPECTING MORE DRAMA.

U-CUT-

KIRKMAN & SCOTT

12-5

THE MOMENT OF TRUTH...
CH LIGHTS
CHRISTMAS LIGHTS

...WHEN WE FIND OUT IF LAST YEAR'S DARRYL PUT THE LIGHTS AWAY NEATLY, OR JUST STUFFED THEM IN THE BOX.
©2021, BABY BLUES BROS LLC DIST. BY KING FEATURES SYNDICATE 12-6

I CAN'T STAND LAST YEAR'S DARRYL.
KIRKMAN & SCOTT

DARRYL, WHERE'S HAMMIE?
HE'S HOLDING THE LADDER FOR ME.

NO, HE'S NOT.
OH.
©2021, BABY BLUES BROS LLC DIST. BY KING FEATURES SYNDICATE 12-7

NO WONDER IT FEELS LESS WOBBLY.
KIRKMAN & SCOTT

WHAT'S THAT IN THE BRANCHES?
WHERE?

HMM...IT'S BROWN AND FURRY.

PROBABLY TOO SMALL TO BE A GRIZZLY.
JUST REACH IN THERE AND GRAB IT!
©2021, BABY BLUES BROS LLC DIST. BY KING FEATURES SYNDICATE 12-8
KIRKMAN & SCOTT

OH, MAN. THERE'S A MOUSE NEST!
DO YOU SEE THE MOUSE?

YEP. THERE HE GOES.
KIRKMAN & SCOTT

IT'S MOVING??
STIRRING.
©2021, BABY BLUES BROS LLC DIST. BY KING FEATURES SYNDICATE 12-9

I CAUGHT THE MOUSE!
ALL RIGHT, DAD!

ARE WE GOING TO STUFF IT AND HANG IT ON THE WALL?
WHAT? NO! WE'RE GOING TO SET IT FREE.
©2021, BABY BLUES BROS LLC DIST. BY KING FEATURES SYNDICATE 12-10

THERE GOES MY CHANCE FOR A TROPHY ROOM.
YOU'LL THANK ME SOMEDAY.
KIRKMAN & SCOTT

THIS IS WHAT ZOE WANTS FOR CHRISTMAS.
GAH!

IT'S CALLED "BABY PONY-FACE."
A DOLL WITH A HORSE'S HEAD? THAT'S DISGUSTING!
©2021, BABY BLUES BROS LLC DIST. BY KING FEATURES SYNDICATE 12-11

IT'S JUST A TOY.
TO PLAY WITH OR HIDE FROM?
KIRKMAN & SCOTT

AAAAND... DONE!

GUYS! IT'S TIME TO PLUG IN THE CHRISTMAS LIGHTS!

THREE! TWO! ONE!

MERRY C—

LET'S GO IN BEFORE WE HEAR ANY NOT-SAFE-FOR-SANTA LANGUAGE.

AW!

KIRKMAN & SCOTT 12-12

SO, WHAT'S THAT THING ZOE WANTS FOR CHRISTMAS?
BABY-PONY-FACE.

IT'S A DOLL WITH A HUMAN BODY AND THE HEAD OF A PONY.

IT CRIES, WHINNIES AND COMES WITH ITS OWN VET BILLS.
WHATEVER HAPPENED TO TEDDY BEARS?
KIRKMAN & SCOTT

SO, I WENT TO THE TOY STORE AND ASKED THE CLERK IF THEY HAD ANY BABY-PONY-FACE DOLLS.
WHAT DID THEY SAY?

BWAHAHAHAHAHAHA!

KIRKMAN & SCOTT
THAT'S A DIRECT QUOTE.
UH-OH.

ZOE WILL BE SO DISAPPOINTED IF SHE DOESN'T GET A BABY-PONY-FACE DOLL FOR CHRISTMAS.
THIS IS CRAZY! EVERYONE'S SOLD OUT.

AH-HA!! FOUND ONE!

THAT'S NOT BABY-PONY-FACE, THAT'S BABY-EEL-FACE.
WHO IS DESIGNING DOLLS THESE DAYS??
©2021, BABY BLUES BROS LLC DIST. BY KING FEATURES SYNDICATE 12-15

LARRY IN ACCOUNTING SAYS HE KNOWS A PLACE THAT HAS SOME BABY-PONY-FACE DOLLS.
ZOE WILL BE SO HAPPY!

HE SAID I SHOULD GO TONIGHT, WHILE THEY'RE STILL IN STOCK.
DO IT!

WHEN DID CHRISTMAS SHOPPING START TO FEEL LIKE A FELONY?
CASH ONLY.
BABY PONYFACE
©2021, BABY BLUES BROS LLC DIST. BY KING FEATURES SYNDICATE 12-16

YOU GOT ONE!
IT WASN'T EASY.
BABY PONYFACE

YOU ARE LOOKING AT THE LAST BABY-PONY-FACE DOLL IN THE STATE.
WOW!
BABY PONYFACE
©2021, BABY BLUES BROS LLC DIST. BY KING FEATURES SYNDICATE 12-17
KIRKMAN & SCOTT

SANTA COMES THROUGH AGAIN!
CAN I AT LEAST GET CREDITED WITH AN ASSIST?

YOU BETTER WATCH OUT, YOU BETTER NOT CRY
YOU BETTER NOT POUT, I'M TELLING YOU WHY...

...SANTA CLAUS IS COMING TO TOWN!
!! !! !!
©2021, BABY BLUES BROS LLC DIST. BY KING FEATURES SYNDICATE 12-18

'TIS THE SEASON FOR EXTORTION.
FALALALA LA-LALALA PBBBTH!
KIRKMAN & SCOTT

...AND A FOOTBALL,
AND A DRONE...

Candles Plus!

MERRY
I'M-SO-OVER-
THIS PANDEMIC-MAS.

BACK
AT YA'.

KIRKMAN & SCOTT

©2021, BABY BLUES BROS LLC DIST. BY KING FEATURES SYNDICATE 12-19

WE NEED TO FIND A LITTLE GIFT FROM YOU TO ZOE.

WHAT ABOUT THIS?
"BOOGER PATROL ZOMBIE ACTION FIGURE"? UM, NO.
©2021, BABY BLUES BROS LLC DIST. BY KING FEATURES SYNDICATE 12-20

I THINK I SEE THE PROBLEM.
YEAH. SHE'S IMPOSSIBLE TO BUY FOR!

HAVE YOU BEEN GOOD THIS YEAR?

©2021, BABY BLUES BROS LLC DIST. BY KING FEATURES SYNDICATE 12-21

IT'S A MATTER OF OPINION.
BASED ON SOME UGLY FACTS!

WHAT'S THIS?
I KNOW YOU'RE BUSY, SO I MADE AN AGENDA.
"DISCUSSION ITEM NUMBER ONE...
"...IS MY BROTHER A BOOGERHEAD?"
I'LL START...
©2021, BABY BLUES BROS LLC DIST. BY KING FEATURES SYNDICATE 12-22
KIRKMAN & SCOTT

I'M LOOKING FOR SOMETHING FOR MY WIFE.
DO YOU KNOW HER SIZE?
YES. YES, I DO.
BUT I'M FORBIDDEN TO SHARE IT.
A BOOK IS ALWAYS NICE.
©2021, BABY BLUES BROS LLC DIST. BY KING FEATURES SYNDICATE 12-23
KIRKMAN & SCOTT

WELL, WE DID IT.

THE KIDS ARE IN BED, AND WE CAN FINALLY GET SOME REST.

©2021, BABY BLUES BROS LLC DIST. BY KING FEATURES SYNDICATE 12-24
HERE'S THE ASSEMBLY STUFF.
SLEEP IS OVERRATED.
KIRKMAN & SCOTT

READY?
READY.

♪♫ WAKE UP, GUYS... IT'S ♪♫ CHRISTMAS MORNING!
KIRKMAN & SCOTT
©2021, BABY BLUES BROS LLC DIST. BY KING FEATURES SYNDICATE 12-25

DID YOU GET THE SHOT?
URG.
RIP!
RIP!
RIP!

WAAAA!
WREN'S DOLL LEG FELL OFF!
HAMMIE SAID BABY PONY FACE IS UGLY!
I GOT ANOTHER CLAMSHELL CUT!
I NEED NEW BATTERIES!
THESE INSTRUCTIONS ARE IN CHINESE!
HAPPY TWENTY-SIXTH.
KIRKMAN & SCOTT

AHHH! ANOTHER WEEK OF HOLIDAY BREAK!
YEP.

CAN I GO OVER TO TRENT'S HOUSE? WE HAVE BIG PLANS.
SUCH AS...?
©2021, BABY BLUES BROS LLC DIST. BY KING FEATURES SYNDICATE 12-27

DREADING GOING BACK TO SCHOOL.
GOOD USE OF YOUR TIME.
KIRKMAN & SCOTT

LUNCHTIME!
KIRKMAN & SCOTT

WHAT IS IT?
I CALL IT "NOONTIME SURPRISE."
©2021, BABY BLUES BROS LLC DIST. BY KING FEATURES SYNDICATE 12-28

THAT MEANS IT'S GROCERY SHOPPING DAY.
REMEMBER THE TIME SHE GAVE US GRAHAM CRACKER AND GRAPE SANDWICHES?

HERE COMES BOBBY.

LET'S GO.
WHERE?

KIRKMAN & SCOTT
I'M GOING TO HAVE A WORD WITH THE KID WHO'S BULLYING YOU!
©2021, BABY BLUES BROS LLC DIST. BY KING FEATURES SYNDICATE 12-31
MOM! NO! IT'LL RUIN MY STREET CRED!
WITH YOU, IT'S MORE CRUD THAN CRED.

THAT'S THE LAST TIME YOU'RE MEAN TO MY SON!
YES, MA'AM! SORRY!

DON'T EVER LET ANYBODY INTIMIDATE YOU, HAMMIE.
OKAY!
©2022, BABY BLUES BROS LLC DIST. BY KING FEATURES SYNDICATE 1-1

ANYBODY BUT ME, THAT IS.
RATS.
KIRKMAN & SCOTT

***Baby Blues***® is distributed internationally by Andrews McMeel Syndication.



Andrews McMeel Publishing
a division of Andrews McMeel Universal
1130 Walnut Street, Kansas City, Missouri 64106

www.andrewsmcmeel.com

22 23 24 25 26 SDB 10 9 8 7 6 5 4 3 2 1

ISBN: 978-1-5248-7562-6

Library of Congress Control Number: 2022935505

Editor: Lucas Wetzel
Designer/Art Director: Julie Barnes
Production Manager: Chadd Keim
Production Editor: Julie Railsback

Find *Baby Blues*® on the Web at www.babyblues.com.

ATTENTION: SCHOOLS AND BUSINESSES
Andrews McMeel books are available at quantity discounts with bulk purchase for educational, business, or sales promotional use. For information, please e-mail the Andrews McMeel Publishing Special Sales Department: specialsales@amuniversal.